THE
PURPOSE-BASED
LIBRARY

THE PURPOSE-BASED LIBRARY

Finding Your Path to Survival, Success, and Growth

JOHN J. HUBER
STEVEN V. POTTER

An imprint of the American Library Association

CHICAGO 2015

ISBN: 978-0-8389-1244-7 (paper)

Library of Congress Cataloging-in-Publication Data

Huber, John J., 1958-
    The purpose-based library : finding your path to survival, success, and growth / John Huber, Steven V. Potter.
      pages   cm
    Includes bibliographical references and index.
    ISBN 978-0-8389-1244-7 (print : alk. paper) 1. Library administration. 2. Libraries—Cost control. 3. Public services (Libraries) 4. Organizational change. 5. Organizational effectiveness. I. Potter, Steven V. II. Title.
    Z678.H844 2015
    025.1—dc23   2014046363

Cover design by Kimberly Thornton. Images © solarseven/Shutterstock, Inc.

Text composition by Dianne M. Rooney in the Chaparral, Gotham, and Bell Gothic typefaces.

♾ This paper meets the requirements of ANSI/NISO Z39.48-1992 (Permanence of Paper).

Printed in the United States of America

19 18 17 16 15   5 4 3 2 1

Contents

Figures and Tables

FIGURES

TABLES

CARRIE COOGAN
Director, CEO of Literacy Kansas City
Missouri

Foreword

Literacy for All

A S A YOUNG CHILD GROWING UP IN A FAMILY OF SEVEN CHIL-
dren, some of my fondest memories are of trips to the library. It happened every week. We would all pile into the car, and that's when my imagination immediately began to run wild with possibilities. What would be happening at the library today? Storytime? Puppet show? Arts and crafts? What interesting books would I find this time tucked away in the shelves? What intriguing places would I visit, what people would I meet, would I learn how to sew or draw, garden, cook a pizza, or write a poem? In a middle-class family of seven children, there are very, very few choices, but at the library the options were endless, exciting, and always an adventure. I could choose anything I wanted to learn or any destination I wanted to travel and meet people from the past or the present. A trip to the library, for me, my brothers and sisters, and yes, even my mom, was a window to the world. A chance to learn, grow, and expand our horizons.

Those days, simple as they sound, have turned out to be the foundation of my education and love of reading.

So when I hear the reports and rumblings of how libraries are fighting extinction and working on ways to stay relevant, it feels heartbreaking, like someone is attacking a cherished friend, a family member, a partner in crime.

Yet, the powerful emergence of technology has forced library leaders to look more closely at how they are serving their clients in a way that continues to be exciting and energizing and bring value to the community. Today, as director of the nonprofit organization Literacy Kansas City, my mission is to help people ages 16 and older learn to read. In this position I now see reading and the vital and critical role of libraries from a much different perspective. The services, programs, and access that libraries can provide through community partnerships are now for many people the *only* resource they may have. At Literacy Kansas City we see every day the struggles that come with illiteracy. Millions of people—one in five in the nation—can't read above a fourth-grade level. As one nonprofit, we can't reach this population alone, but we can make a difference, reach them in their neighborhoods where they feel most comfortable and familiar, and change lives—with the help of libraries. Libraries provide the infrastructure, resources, outreach, technology, and the open, welcoming arms that people who can't read so desperately need. The libraries of today, through creative collaboration with nonprofit organizations like Literacy Kansas City, provide a whole new model for community learning. In our partnerships with the local libraries we are able to reach families, teens, and adults where they live. At neighborhood libraries Literacy Kansas City provides computer-based digital and literacy skills classes enabling both adult and teen students to learn how to read while using a computer. We teach reading, writing, financial, and digital life skills, as well as facilitate tutoring and family reading programs. Other nonprofits need the libraries to help deliver their services to other clients, like English language learners and senior citizens, and provide workforce readiness skills classes as well as GED courses. Strong partnerships allow libraries and nonprofits to focus on and provide the services they need at a particular branch or community—one area may not need a heavy dose of digital life skills classes for senior citizens but they may desperately need a program for adult literacy classes. Not only does this allow libraries and nonprofits to work in concert to serve the needs of their clients where they are, but it's more efficient, as resources and staff are shared and services aren't being duplicated. The programs fit the needs of the people and, with collaboration and partnerships, libraries become the nerve centers and hubs that help build stronger, smarter communities and, where needed, provide a way out of illiteracy and poverty for their citizens.

Today, I see our library leaders not struggling with, but adapting to this time of change and working on ways to face it head on. John Huber and Steve Potter provide a framework for libraries to continue to lead into the 21st century by being lean, flexible, and adaptable and on a never-ending quest to serve the needs of the community in a valuable way. They are creating a vision that shows how libraries are now more vital than ever when it comes to uniting and lifting a community up and infusing a lifelong love of learning into every citizen.

JOHN J. HUBER

Introduction

It was the best of times, it was the worst of times, it was the age of wisdom, it was the age of foolishness, it was the epoch of belief, it was the epoch of incredulity, it was the season of Light, it was the season of Darkness, it was the spring of hope, it was the winter of despair, we had everything before us, we had nothing before us . . . .

—Charles Dickens, *A Tale of Two Cities*

ONE MIGHT ARGUE THAT REDUCED BUDGETS, AGGRESSIVE competition, the rapid pace of technology, management outsourcing, unfriendly publishers, skeptical city managers, and ever-increasing customer expectations have created "the worst of times" for libraries. In this book we propose that libraries are poised to create "the best of times." Before we explore this potential, let us first examine the state of our current times. During my travels across North America I have seen firsthand the challenges libraries face. Here are a few news clippings that document the struggles.

Toronto

Last year [2011] the Toronto Public Library was asked by Mayor Rob Ford to cut its $170 million operating budget by 10 percent, or $17 million. The mayor said the city needed to make drastic budget cuts due to financial concerns. At one point, the library faced a possible 7 percent cut to operating hours, branch closures, more job cuts, and a 27 percent cut to the collections budget.[1]

Texas

Two years ago, when Texas was confronting a $27 billion budget short-fall, state lawmakers chain-sawed the 2012–13 funding for the Texas State Library and Archives Commission by 64 percent. Now that cut may be creating an even more dire financial problem for libraries. Since the state isn't meeting its mandated share of funding, the federal government is threatening to cut nearly 70 percent of its annual funding for Texas public libraries, saying the state has failed to pull its own weight. "It does kind of hit us with a double whammy," said Mark Smith, director of the commission, which provides support for 560 libraries statewide.[2]

California

New California Gov. Jerry Brown, facing tremendous budget problems, has proposed a statewide budget that eliminates state spending on public libraries entirely. Those cuts amount to around $30 million.[3]

Kansas

Kansas has sharply reduced state support for schools, libraries, and other community services in recent years, forcing towns and cities to cut programs that Kansans depend upon or raise more money locally to sustain them. While the cuts by the state were initially prompted by the Great Recession, the substantial income tax cuts Kansas lawmakers enacted in 2012 and 2013 are draining even more resources and making it nearly impossible to replace vital aid to Kansas communities. State support for libraries has been cut by over 30 percent, forcing reductions in operating hours, cutbacks in book purchases, or the establishment of waiting lists for summer reading programs. In some areas, libraries are the only resource many people have for filling out online job applications and furthering their education.[4]

New York

For the first time, the 62 branches in the borough [of Queens] have stopped buying new books in order to save costs. "This is by far the worst we've ever seen it," said Thomas Galante, the chief executive officer for the Queens Library. Overall, city libraries are facing nearly

$100 million in budget cuts, which they say would lead to an estimated 1,500 layoffs. The proposed steep reductions would cripple the system, advocates say.[5]

Colorado

The [Denver Public] Library Commission recommends pursuing branch closures to maintain minimum service standards, and with a $2.5 million reduction in the budget, this would mean 7–12 branches would close indefinitely.[6]

Nationwide

A private company [Library Systems & Services (LSSI)] in Maryland has taken over public libraries in ailing cities in California, Oregon, Tennessee, and Texas, growing into the country's fifth-largest library system.[7]

In the face of these setbacks, libraries and their supporters are not sitting on their hands and just giving up. They have responded. As Paul Harvey used to say, "Here is the rest of the story."

Toronto

More than 30,000 people signed a petition protesting the library cuts and several thousand people spoke out against cuts at the December library board meeting and through e-mails sent to the City Council.[8]

Texas

The Texas State Library and Archives Commission (TSLAC) successfully appealed an October 2013 decision by the Institute of Museum and Library Services (IMLS), restoring $6.5 million in federal matching funds designated to support library activities across the Lone Star State.[9]

Colorado

On Monday, August 20, City Council voted 11–1 to refer a measure to the November ballot asking voters to [circumvent mandated cuts in city property tax established by the Tax Payer's Bill of Rights (TABOR)]. This measure, [named for TABOR's sponsor, Douglas Bruce, and] commonly known as "de-Brucing" would allow Denver to retain what it already collects under current tax rates, taking Denver out from under a state-mandated spending cap formula in TABOR. By removing the TABOR spending limits, the city will have an additional $68 million dollars to improve police and fire protection, repair city streets and restore Library hours.[10]

These victories are a few good signs, but as we all know, Pandora's box has been opened. Budget issues will keep libraries in the spotlight, and library relevancy will continue to be an accepted topic at social gatherings. When I tell people I am a library consultant, I often hear the following responses.

"Why do we need to provide books and DVDs to people who can afford to buy them?"

"Why do we need reference librarians when we have Google?"

"I buy my e-books from Amazon because my library cannot keep up."

"Bookstores are going out of business, are libraries next?"

"Do we really need libraries anymore?"

The answer? We need libraries now more than ever.

As they say in my home state of Oklahoma, this is not my first rodeo. During the 1980s and 1990s, I served as a service and process improvement consultant for a manufacturing industry fighting to survive. It was my job to help my clients survive global outsourcing, labor cuts, union/management labor battles, and big-box-driven price deflation. Many asked at the time whether US manufacturing could survive. The answer is many companies did and many did not. From my experience, those who survived fully embraced a concept called "lean manufacturing," or "lean." Lean preaches a philosophy that those within an organization must squeeze out all the waste in their operation. If they do not, their competitors will by default.

I have been a pioneer in the lean manufacturing movement since 1981, and in 2001, I had the unique opportunity to introduce the concept of lean to the Tulsa City-County library, my local library. Since that game-changing day, our 13-year partnership has developed some groundbreaking ideas on how to remove waste from library service delivery chains. I have since had the privilege of introducing lean to libraries across North America. The results have been dramatic:

Holds delivery performance improved to same day/next day delivery while reducing costs by 20 to 33 percent for Pikes Peak Library District, Tulsa City-County Library, Public Library of Youngstown and Mahoning County (OH), Southern Maryland Regional Library Association, Western Maryland Library Association, and Austin (TX) Public Library.

New book receipt-to-shelf lead time was reduced by 50 to 75 percent with a 10 to 33 percent reduction in cost for Pikes Peak Library District, Kansas City (MO) Public Library, Tulsa City-County Library, Pueblo (CO) City/County Library District, and Houston (TX) Public Library.

Holds processing clerical support cost was reduced by 25 to 33 percent at Johnson County (KS) Library, Kansas City Public Library, Tulsa City-

County Library, Ottawa Public Library, Fort Worth Library, Fairfax County (VA) Public Library, and Austin Public Library.

A process innovation implemented at Missouri's Mid-Continent Public Library (MCPL), the "holds label solution," reduced clerical activities by the equivalent of 17 full-time employees (FTEs). MCPL was able to staff an entire new library branch with the savings.

Tote box use was eliminated in the delivery process, cutting 98 percent of required heavy lifting, at Tulsa City-County Library, Public Library of Youngstown and Mahoning, and Anoka County (MN) Library System.

These experiences and many more inspired me to share my Lean Library methodology and our success stories by writing my first book, *Lean Library Management: Eleven Strategies for Reducing Costs and Improving Customer Services*. In simple terms, common management thinking states that if budgets are reduced, customer service suffers. Lean states that if you streamline and improve customer services and therefore eliminate wasteful activities, costs will go down. I believe, and all the libraries listed above believe, that they must embrace Lean Library Management to survive. My experience in both the manufacturing and library worlds supports this premise.

In chapter 1, we further explore Lean Library survival by examining a case study of Carrollton (TX) Public Library (CPL). CPL was at risk of being outsourced to the LSSI management group, and by embracing the concepts of Lean, CPL's independence survived.

After I wrote *Lean Library Management*, I had a nagging feeling that the lean survival message, while critical, represents only part of the competitive solution for libraries. The truth, as you know, is that libraries are more than just book distributors; libraries influence their community as a whole by providing critical and value-added services. I fear that under the pressure of decreased budgets, increased competition, and skeptical city managers, libraries will soon be reduced to only core distribution services. I fear libraries will be forced to lose sight of their real purpose. This would be a huge mistake, not only from a social fabric viewpoint but also from a business competition viewpoint. Library services that go beyond book distribution differentiate you from your competition, and therefore provide you a distinct competitive advantage. Properly embraced, measured, and marketed, these unique services can take your library beyond survival to a competitive path of success and growth. The only way for libraries to survive the intense competition of Barnes & Noble, Amazon, Netflix, and Google (what I call the BANG group) is to become as lean as possible while also offering value-added services beyond what the BANG group, or for that matter anyone else, can provide.

Libraries find themselves at a critical juncture. Do libraries continue to separate themselves from their customers through customer self-service models in order to compete with the likes of the BANG group? Or do libraries look within themselves to embrace their true purpose and use this purpose to create a more effective competitive business model? Can libraries realign their staff and their skills along this new model? Can they embrace change?

Over dinner one night Steven Potter, director of the Mid-Continent Public Library, and I discussed these questions and examined the path libraries are currently traveling, and we shared our visions for a different path. It turns out we had very similar ideas, which motivated us to collaborate on this book. We believe:

- Survival depends on quicker, faster, better lean core services.
- Success depends on community/library partnerships and value-added metrics.
- Growth depends on libraries communicating, reflecting, and pursuing their true purpose.

In this book, we will cover each of these topics.

In part I we address survival and the concept of Lean Library Management. We present a case study in chapter 1 where one library took action to control their fate and survived another day.

Part II presents our vision beyond survival toward success and growth. In chapter 2 we discuss the need to rethink our traditional metrics of circulation and budgets and embrace metrics that better reflect your library's real purpose. Chapter 3 examines the paradox between libraries pursuing their true mission and purpose versus the current direction of customer self-driven services. We also discuss the considerable footprint libraries have in this country and the leverage this implies. Chapter 4 introduces the community pyramid that will drive our purpose-based library. Chapter 5 seeks to define what a community is and explores its relationship with its local library. In chapters 6 through 16, we examine the community pyramid, delving into the current state of each pyramid's step and the role libraries can play to prioritize and impact the health and well-being of each step.

Part III goes beyond survival and success and presents our vision for growth. In chapter 17 we discuss the retention and realignment of library resources to better reflect the purpose-based library. Chapter 18 presents a new vision for a value-added market strategy. In chapter 19 we discuss how the purpose-based library can be more effective in attracting philanthropic resources. Chapter 20 outlines how the purpose-based library should align their physical presentation with their true purpose. In chapter 21 we propose libraries embrace the concept of supporting self-published authors through library publishing services and the need for consolidated buying groups.

Part IV covers sustainability. In chapter 22 we discuss the need for the members within a community to sustain their pyramid.

Each chapter is written from my voice (John Huber). And at the end of each chapter, the book presents Potter's Perspective, Points, and Ponderings, where Steve provides his unique thoughts on the topic presented.

Steve and I appreciate your interest in these topics. This book is certainly not the last word, but we are compelled to start or join the conversation, as we believe libraries must not only survive, but look to a future of success and growth. We believe the path we present will usher in a new era for libraries, an era when libraries can say, "It is the best of times."

NOTES

1. Michelle Lee, "Toronto Public Library Manages to Avoid Steeper Cut," *Library Journal*, February 7, 2012, http://lj.libraryjournal.com/2012/02/funding/toronto-public-library-manages-to-avoid-steeper-cut.
2. Steve Campbell and Edgar Walters, "Texas Public Libraries Face 70% Cut in Federal Funding," *Star-Telegram/The Texas Tribune*, November 8, 2013.
3. Carolyn Kellogg, "Brown's Proposed Budget Eliminates State Funding for Public Libraries" *Los Angeles Times*, January 12, 2011, http://latimesblogs.latimes.com/jacketcopy/2011/01/brown-budget-eliminates-california-library-funding.html#sthash.nIVdGAMW.dpuf.
4. "Who Pays? The Cost of Kansas' Tax Cuts for Local Communities," Kansas Center for Economic Growth (2013), http://realprosperityks.com/kac/wp-content/uploads/2013/12/KS-Center-for-Economic-Growth-Local-Impacts-Report.pdf.
5. Reuvan Blau, "Funding Cuts Closing Book on All 62 branches in Queens Library," *Daily News*, May 24, 2011, www.nydailynews.com/new-york/queens/funding-cuts-closing-book-62-branches-queens-library-article-1.141568#ixzz2wLYfpUEx.
6. Shirley Amore, "Denver Public Library Prepares for a Potential $2.5 Million Budget Cut," Denver Public Library blog, April 21, 2011, http://denverlibrary.org/budget-cut.
7. David Streitfeld, "Anger as a Private Company Takes Over Libraries," *New York Times*, September 26, 2010, www.nytimes.com/2010/09/27/business/27libraries.html?pagewanted=all.
8. Lee, "Toronto Public Library Manages to Avoid Steeper Cut."
9. Ian Chant, "Texas Successfully Appeals IMLS Funding Cuts," *Library Journal*, January 21, 2014, http://lj.libraryjournal.com/2014/01/budgets-funding/texas-successfully-appeals-imls-funding-cuts.
10. Eli Stokols, "Denver Council Sends Measure to 'de-Bruce' Property Taxes to Voters," Fox 31 Denver, August 20, 2012, http://kdvr.com/2012/08/20/denver-council-sends-measure-to-de-bruce-property-taxes-to-voters.

PART I

Survival

For those who have attended one of my workshops or have read my first book, you are familiar with a story I tell called "My Honeymoon Kitchen." For those who know the story, bear with me, as there are a few updates.

I graduated college with an industrial engineering and management degree and was hired by Accenture Consulting (formerly Andersen Consulting). My wife, Kathy, worked at the American Association of Petroleum Geologists assisting the group to plan their annual conventions.

One day I came home from work a bit late, sat down at the kitchen table, and watched Kathy cook our evening meal, spaghetti with meat sauce. I watched her go to the refrigerator for onions, to the utensil drawer for a knife, to the cabinet for a pan, back to the refrigerator for hamburger meat, to the pantry for spaghetti sauce, back to the utensil drawer for a spoon, back to the pantry for salt, back to the cabinet for a saucepan, back to the pantry for pepper—well, you get the idea.

I voiced my thoughts, "You know, honey, if you just planned out ahead of time what you need, you could get everything together ahead of time and save yourself a lot of time."

When I get to this point in my story, you can see the daggers in the eyes of all my female participants. Well, I did save my wife a lot of time cooking, as she told me I would be cooking dinner for now on. (That lasted about two weeks until she got tired of Hamburger Helper.)

You have to forgive me, for as an industrial engineer, I cannot go anywhere without seeing improvement opportunities. I see it in fast-food restaurants, retail stores, workers on the highway, and yes, my manufacturing, distribution, and library clients.

The real lesson I learned from my honeymoon kitchen is that people don't like other people coming into their kitchen and telling them what to do. For the past 35 years of my consulting career, I have carried that lesson with me constantly. I understand that your library is your kitchen, and Steve and I are not here to tell you how to run your kitchen. However, these are serious times for libraries and it is important that each of you take a new look at your kitchen and challenge yourself to see the opportunities that exist, and believe me, they exist. Our objective is to provide you ideas and case studies on survival and a vision beyond survival toward success and growth. By reading this book, you have invited us into your kitchen, and we thank you for the invite. We will try to be good guests.

I have an update to my honeymoon kitchen story. I was talking with a librarian about what I do as a consultant, and she asked me if I had ever heard of Frank and Lillian Gilbreth. Well, I certainly had heard of Frank Gilbreth, as his efficiency work and time study methodology is taught to all industrial engineers. What I did not know was the story of Lillian Gilbreth. Frank and Lillian had 12 children, and Lillian was Frank's partner in his management-consulting firm, Gilbreth, Inc. The original movie *Cheaper by the Dozen* (not the one with Steve Martin) was based on Frank and Lillian's book by the same title. The movie tells the story of how they efficiently organized their kids, themselves, and their daily tasks to survive the day. Ironically, Lillian even wrote many books and articles on the topics of kitchen efficiency. So, perhaps I was channeling Lillian those many years ago.

I do differ a bit from the Gilbreths. While they focused on the efficiency of a task, I focus on the overall speed and quality of a service event. I believe your survival depends on first and foremost streamlining your service delivery chains, a topic we will address in detail in the following chapter.

1
Lean Library Management

COMMUNITY TRANSFORMATION IS AT THE HEART OF EVERY library and is the focus of this book. However, before libraries can embrace the strategy we propose, they must survive the current environment of budget cuts and staff reductions. In this chapter you will learn how to survive. You will be introduced to the transformational power of Lean Library Management. You will discover that lean is simple in concept, powerful in practice. You will see through an actual case study that transforming your library to a lean culture can be managed, controlled, and implemented through a standard lean transformational methodology.

Lean Library Management: Eleven Strategies for Reducing Costs and Improving Customer Services, my previous book, presents a step-by-step strategy for how to integrate the concepts of lean into your library—in other words, how to become quicker, faster, better. Many of you have embraced my book, and I thank you for the great feedback and encouragement.

To understand lean, imagine you are about to embark on a great river adventure. In front of you are two boats from which you must choose. One boat is very large and bulky. It looks safe, but it looks as if it is in need of repair. The other boat is smaller and sleeker in design. You have never seen anything like this boat. You have limited funds and a limited crew. Despite your limitations, the river adventure you are about to embark upon will present unpredictable currents, hidden rocks, flooding, and white waters. You know this adventure will require a strong, responsive boat with a small but experienced crew. You quickly realize that the larger boat, while providing a sense of security, will ride low in the water, will be slow and sluggish in response to changing conditions, and may very well get stuck in the mud in low-water conditions. The choice is clear: the smaller boat better fits the size of your crew; is easier to navigate; is more responsive to the changing currents, hidden rocks, and shallow waters; and most important, is more agile.

You have the same choice with your library. Do you choose a large, bulky, unresponsive library, or do you choose a more streamlined, responsive library, one that is strong in its core services and capable of redirecting its path at a moment's notice? The truth is that you have no choice. The current economic conditions, reduced budgets, reduced staff, and more limited services have forced you into the smaller boat—or worse, the larger boat with a skeleton crew. However, even if the economic conditions were different, you would still be better served by choosing the more streamlined boat because it provides better services to your customers and has a better chance to respond to changing conditions.

Many believe tighter budgets (smaller boat and crew) lead to poorer customer service. Lean teaches us the exact opposite. If you improve and streamline your customer service, you become quicker, faster, better. Improve service, and you reduce costs. By embracing lean and streamlining your processes, you will be traveling in the smaller, more responsive boat on a straight, smooth, fast-flowing river.

I will not duplicate the presentation of my lean strategies in this book, however I would encourage you to seek out *Lean Library Management* to further explore lean concepts, as they are critical to your short-term survival. To illustrate this point, we will review a case study of a library whose future was in doubt and that embraced the concepts of lean to survive another day.

CARROLLTON PUBLIC LIBRARY—CASE STUDY

Carrollton Public Library, a two-branch library system located about 20 miles north of Dallas, supports a collection of about 186,000, circulates about 750,000 items annually, and has a staff of 37.5 FTEs, while serving a population of about 121,000 residents.

In 2011, I conducted a series of lean workshops for the (former) Northeast Texas Library System (NETLS). Many representatives from the Dallas community libraries attended, including from Carrollton Public. The workshops provided the participants an introductory understanding of the power of Lean Library Management, including the following best practice service improvement concepts:

- Lean is like a smooth flowing river I call the River Lean. The River Lean has smooth banks and steady flowing water with clear sailing ahead. Most organizations travel Snake River on a large, heavy boat attempting to navigate twists and turns (poor flow), destructive hidden rocks (inefficiencies), and periods of dry and muddy river beds (imbalances), followed by intense flooding (peak loads). Lean pursues a smaller, fast-traveling boat on a smooth flowing river.
- Lean sees your library as a series of service delivery chains (SDCs), not segmented departments or staff.
- Lean teaches us that measurements drive and feed your service performance; therefore, what you do not measure must not be important.
- Lean knows that waste exists in every service process a library supports.
- Lean shows us that service improvement leads to dramatic cost reduction.

Two major factors drove CPL to attend this workshop. First, when it comes to reducing wasteful costs, Carrollton's city council is a very serious group. As far back as 2002, the city implemented what they call a "managed competition" program whereby each of the city's service groups is targeted for a competitive review. Of the 11 service groups reviewed thus far, four had been outsourced. CPL was next on the managed competition list. One can only be impressed with Carrollton's managed competition program. In the words of Tom Guilfoy, director of managed competition for the City of Carrollton, "Carrollton's 10-year-old 'managed competition' program has resulted in $30 million in various one-time and ongoing savings over the years (out of a general fund budget of $74 million)."

Second, to make things even more exciting, just five miles up the road the Farmers Branch City Council and mayor sparked controversy when they turned over the management reins of their one-branch community library to LSSI, a for-profit management group. Carrollton knew that to survive they had to not only reduce costs but also improve customer service.

In the words of Lynette Jones, CPL public services supervisor, "Staff had witnessed other city departments work through the process and either win (be declared Substantially Competitive) or lose (get outsourced to a private vendor), and everyone knew that we were playing for high stakes (life and civilization as we know it)."

After the NETLS workshop, CPL's leadership team approached me and requested a follow-up workshop focused on their library. We conducted the workshop a few weeks later, and it was a great success. We reviewed their service delivery chains via the videos they had developed, exposed many wasteful activities, and built great momentum and enthusiasm toward eliminating this waste. After the workshop, CPL prepared for their managed competition review, starting by establishing their driving objectives:

- To be declared substantially competitive (i.e., avoid being outsourced).
- To look at every procedure and process, analyze them, and find ways to improve.
- To leverage technology in the most cost-effective way possible.

In the words of Cherri Gross, former CPL director, "We began our Managed Competition process by conducting a SWOT analysis (Strengths, Weaknesses, Opportunities, and Threats), assigning an EOT (Employee Operations Team), and then using Mr. Huber's methodology to evaluate each one of our service delivery chains. Smaller teams were assigned a service delivery chain, and an action plan was developed. The Library Management Team prioritized the services in the action plan."

Let us briefly explore this best practice concept of SDCs. SDCs represent the series of process events (from beginning to end) that provide an end product or service to your customer. As summarized in my book *Lean Library Management*,

TABLE 1.1

Targeted service delivery chains

Customer Holds SDC	Signs and Verbiage SDC
Customer Service Desk SDC	Grant Acquisition SDC
New Book SDC	Computer Assistance SDC
Self-Check SDC	Circulation SDC
Security SDC	Weeding/Disposal of Withdrawn SDC
Staffing/Scheduling SDC	Phone SDC
Customer Notification SDC	Donations SDC
Materials Returns Check-in SDC	Volunteer SDC
Lost and Paid SDC	Customer and Staff Emergency SDC
Fax SDC	New Books in Transit SDC
Easy Books SDC	Story Time SDC
Scanning and Printing SDC	E-book SDC
Magazine SDC	Coffee Shop SDC
Newspaper SDC	Teen Services SDC
Computer Class SDC	Adult Programming SDC

While libraries are organized and managed within departments or functions, this does not truly reflect the actual flow of services you provide. In fact, department walls can actually inhibit your ability to provide low-cost, high levels of service. The survival of any business lies in its ability to effectively service their customers and to do it in the shortest time at the lowest costs possible. When the separate processes that link together to create this service are separated and managed separately by different groups, the forest can easily be lost among the trees. Library Lean teaches us to ignore the department walls and organizational chart and recognize and document what the true service delivery chain is.[1]

Table 1.1 provides a list of SDCs CPL defined, measured, and attacked.

Performing their SDC analysis over a period of about a year, the assigned teams incorporated J. Huber & Associates lean methodology as summarized in table 1.2.

CPL identified their core services (SDCs), prioritized them, and attacked each one with the objective to improve customer service and eliminate waste. The following sections summarize their SDC accomplishments.

TABLE 1.2

Lean methodology

Sequence	Action Item
I	Identify your SDCs as well as your SDCs' performance objectives.
II	Prioritize your improvement focus and assign cross-functional teams to these priority SDCs. (Carrollton decided to attack them all!)
III	Flowchart/Diagram your SDC so that everyone on the team understands how the overall process works.
IV	Measure how the SDC is performing in terms of service, costs, safety, and quality.
V	Conduct benchmarking and competitor analysis to challenge "in the box" thinking.
VI	Challenge every step of the process to improve service lead times (speeding up the flow of the "river").
VII	Video key process links to examine the waste. Attack waste through brainstorming sessions.
VIII	Prioritize your improvement ideas.
IX	Perform a cost-benefit analysis of your new design concepts.
X	Pilot your ideas to assure success.
XI	Implement performance metrics to assure the SDCs meet your performance objectives.
XII	Attack all performance gaps again and again.

Customer Holds Service Delivery Chain

CPL's Holds SDC team embraced one of my lean concepts I call the "First Touch Rule," which states, if you can perform a task the first time you touch it, do it, because it will eliminate tasks throughout the rest of the process. My Holds Label Solution does just that by combining the pick list, in-transit slip, and the holds slip into one removable label. In other words, the staff person pulling the hold uses the label to find the book on the shelf and then applies that label onto the spine of the book the first time the book is touched. This eliminates the in-transit slip and holds slip activities later in the process. CPL embraced the "First Touch" concept, and as a result, the team freed up 256 clerical hours per year while reducing the time to get the book to the holds shelf by 25 percent.

New Book Service Delivery Chain

CPL's most dramatic impact on service as well as cost came from the New Book SDC team. The New Book SDC team reduced new book delivery times by 95 percent (from two to three months to one week) and reduced staffing by 50 percent (from six staff employees to three) by implementing cost-effective vendor delivery of cataloging and processing services, reducing manual invoice data entry through electronic ordering/invoice consolidation and implementing vendor-generated bar codes and list prices in records.

Customer Service Desk Service Delivery Chain

The Customer Service Desk SDC team soon discovered there was much more to their service chain than just one overall flow. To fully define customer service, the team identified additional SDC flows as shown in table 1.3.

Using the Library Lean best practice tools of flowcharting, videotaping, and brainstorming, the team discovered their current two-desk approach (one for circulation support and one for information/reference support) created a great deal of waste, including duplication of tasks, separation of staff during peak load times, customer confusion, and congestion in the main traffic areas.

TABLE 1.3

Customer service desk SDCs

Detail Service Flows	
Study Room SDC	Check-in SDC
Library Card SDC	Paying Fines SDC
Holds Pickup SDC	Print Cards SDC
Guest Pass SDC	Computer Access Request SDC

The videos revealed many opportunities for improvement. The team identified many service benefits by consolidating the two desks into one:

- eliminated customer confusion while providing a better service experience
- improved peak load service response by better utilizing cross-trained and consolidated staff
- improved staff productivity by eliminating duplicative steps
- improved productivity of staff off-line duties

The one-desk concept improved productivity by 33 percent while eliminating extra walking time and congestion for both the customer and the staff.

Children's Services Delivery Chain

The Children's SDC team identified the need to evaluate their current strategies against a for-profit competitor. This is, after all, what the managed competition program is all about. The group researched local bookstores to see how they support children's services. The team found that the bookstores had advanced sign-up, shorter programs than the library, programs in Spanish, craft and coloring, use of Nooks, Kids Clubs, and paid book performers.

And they did not stop there; the team moved forward by benchmarking themselves against the local school district's curriculum. As a result the Children's SDC team created new and innovative programs more aligned with customer and community needs. CPL believes this will result in better storytimes that will have a lasting impact on the children and their parents.

The following provides additional highlights of other CPL SDC team accomplishments:

The **Grant Acquisition SDC Team** formed by library staff and Parks/ Recreation staff banded together to form the Leisure Services Grant Team. The library applied for five different grants in fiscal year 2011/2012 and received funding from two of those sources.

The **e-book SDC Team** added 515 targeted e-book offerings.

The **Reference SDC Team** targeted and added 24 homework and medical virtual reference books to enhance 24/7 research assistance.

The **Computer Class SDC Team** added 88 volunteer-based computer lab and training programs for Microsoft Word, Excel, and PowerPoint as well as resume writing and job hunting.

On March 6, 2012, CPL was declared substantially competitive. In the words of Carrollton City Manager Leonard Martin, "Anyone can do more with more. It takes a leader and manager to do more with less. And that's where our (library) people are."

CPL not only survived as a management team, but they have become a much stronger library. By strengthening their core services, they are now riding on a smaller, sleeker, and more responsive boat on a river that has fewer twists and turns, fewer hidden rocks, and reduced flooding. They have an experienced and motivated crew and are much better positioned to handle the unpredictable waters they may face in the future.

Libraries across the country, such as Pikes Peak Library District, Mid-Continent Public Library, Cincinnati Public Library, Kansas City Public Library, Fort Worth Public Library, Tulsa City-County Public Library, Public Library of Youngstown/Mahoney County, Humboldt County (CA) Library, Carrollton Public, Austin Public Library, Fairfax County Library, and Sno-Isle (WA) Libraries to just name a few are embracing the Lean Library Methodology. Their objective is to become quicker, faster, better at their core services. As the Carrollton case study shows, libraries cannot take the status quo as a given.

City and county managers as well as the public are questioning the value libraries provide for the cost invested. For the purpose-based library to ultimately succeed and grow, it must first survive. Libraries must show to their communities that they are substantially competitive from a "for profit" viewpoint. They must embrace lean and streamline their core processes by eliminating waste, thus improving customer service, which naturally leads to reduced costs. Libraries must build a smaller, leaner ship to navigate the turbulent and unpredictable waters ahead. They must man their ship with a smaller crew, but a crew that is highly experienced and motivated to succeed.

POTTER'S PERSPECTIVE, POINTS, AND PONDERINGS

A BBC report stated, "Libraries have been failing the public by providing them with often old and incomplete collections. . . . visitor numbers have halved since 1984 and, if this trend continues, people will stop using UK libraries in the next 20 years."[2]

Perhaps Great Britain is the canary in the coal mine for North American libraries. The canary is telling us that libraries must change and adapt, for maintaining the status quo will only lead to irrelevance.

In the introduction, John presented our three-part vision of survival, success, and growth. Survival, the first of which, we address in this chapter. CPL met their managed competition challenge (a challenge we all share whether we want to admit it or not) by looking outside their own four walls for best practices and service principles.

At Mid-Continent, we have done the same, and John has been an important part of our journey. His experience with the manufacturing and distribution industries as well as the library world well positions him to help us look outside ourselves and challenge the status quo. I invited John into our library to help us question the conventional wisdom around our service events. He challenged us to streamline our service flows, employ "first touch" principles, and consider all processes as being in a state of perpetual beta. Nothing is carved in stone. Everything has to be quicker, faster, and better. Our first project resulted in $600,000 in operational savings annually. Another way to look at it is that MCPL decreased the work at our branches by about 17 FTE. We translated these savings by moving those freed-up positions to staff a brand new library service outlet. Imagine opening a new library without any added labor costs. That's what lean and quicker, better, faster did for us and can do for you as well.

You may be thinking that no one is challenging your library like Carrollton Public Library. You may be right. Mid-Continent is autonomous and has its own dedicated funding. The chances that someone will come to our library board and mandate improvement are not very high. However, outside factors like decreasing assessed valuation can drive down library revenues. Sometimes you might want to implement something new. But, because resources are finite, to do something new you will have to stop doing something else. The latter has been more frequently the case at MCPL. Regardless of the motive, lean can be a very effective strategy.

Like our process improvements projects at Mid-Continent, John and I have collaborated throughout this book. Potter's Perspective, Points, and Ponderings are intended to ground our collaboration squarely in the reality of the library world. We did not want this book to be an academic exercise, but a real conversation of action.

In that light, the question posed in this chapter for your library is will you ride the wave of change or be swept under by the tide of change? As a first step of action, I highly recommend you read John's book, *Lean Library Management*, so you too can sail to a future of relevance by navigating a more streamlined and responsive boat.

NOTES

1. John J. Huber, *Lean Library Management: Eleven Strategies for Reducing Costs and Improving Customer Services* (New York: Neal-Schuman, 2011).
2. "UK Libraries Out of Use by 2020," BBC News, April 27, 2004, http://news .bbc.co.uk/go/pr/fr/-/2/hi/uk_news/3661831.stm.

PART II

Success

The most meaningful way to differentiate your company from your competitors, the best way to put distance between you and the crowd is to do an outstanding job with information. How you gather, manage, and use information will determine whether you win or lose.

—Bill Gates

Bill Gates's quote should have you, as a member of the library profession, doing backflips. Librarians are specifically trained to gather, manage, and use information. Therefore, if we take Bill Gates's words at face value, libraries should be the most competitive organizations on the planet. Some of you would argue that your library is a nonprofit organization and is not competing with anyone. I beg to differ. Every customer has a choice and chooses whether to go to the library website or Google's search bar, to either engage the library or order materials from Amazon.com. Amazon would much rather have its customers buy a book than borrow, and Google would much rather have information seekers search its website than seek out a reference or research librarian (or for that matter a library "deep web" research database).

FIGURE II.1
Competitive differentiation

There is no question that libraries compete head to head with these for-profit businesses.

Figure II.1 presents a Venn diagram of the competitive overlaps between libraries, Google, and Netflix.

Libraries are competing against the most successful businesses this planet has ever seen, and considering this competition, libraries have responded admirably. Embracing self-service technology, adopting one-field deep-web database search engines, expanding e-book offerings, creating staff-less libraries, and streamlining service-delivery chains by embracing the concepts of Lean Library Management are a few examples. However, libraries must face the reality that they have an uphill battle competing with these very impressive and highly profit-driven companies. Google has for the most part won the "surface web" battle, as the role of the reference librarian has become a shell of itself. Amazon is winning the battle for e-books, primarily because of their effective user interface, wealth of offerings, and their easy-to-use digital delivery platform (not to mention publishers' e-book pricing models favoring Amazon). Nonetheless, libraries are hanging in there and competing effectively, but for how long? They are surviving, but survival is not enough—success and growth have to be a part of libraries' survival strategies or they will eventually lose their relevance. To successfully compete against the likes of Amazon, Google, and Netflix, libraries must embrace the words of Bill Gates. Libraries must gather, use, and manage information in a way that large for-profit companies cannot. So the question is, what do libraries have that these organizations do not? What competitive advantage can they possibly have? Let us count the ways:

- Libraries have more locations across the country than any other organization.
- Libraries have a personal presence in every community in the country.
- Libraries interact with their customers face-to-face.
- Libraries are trained and skilled to gather, archive, and manage information.
- Library staffs are very well-educated and motivated to make a difference.
- And most important, libraries and their staff have a powerful game-changing common purpose.

To go beyond survival, to succeed and grow, libraries must embrace and leverage these competitive advantages. Steve and I believe we have provided a road map to do just that. In part II we unveil the road map to success, in part III we reveal the road map to growth, and in part IV we discuss sustainability.

2
Good Morning

M Y FAVORITE PART OF MY LEAN WORKSHOPS IS WHEN I ASK
the participants to write down on an index card why they chose the
library for a profession. The answers can be quite funny. "My mother made me
do it" is my favorite. Most of the responses follow a theme: "I like helping people," "I like connecting people to information," and "I like serving my community." After about 15 minutes of the group sharing their own stories, I ask the
group, "Did anyone write down 'I chose the library profession to increase circulation and reduce budgets?'" It draws a big laugh, but it is a serious question.
In this chapter you will discover how circulation and budgets do not properly
reflect your library's true purpose or your true purpose.

If you are reading this book, you are one of those who has dedicated much
of your life to helping people. It is why you get up in the morning. A few years
ago I was riding along with the director of a Maryland county library. As I
often do, I asked her why she became a librarian. She told me that when she
was a child she had a very mean librarian. She was very aware of the impact
this librarian had on the children around her. Rather than focusing on the
negative side of what she and her friends experienced, she focused on the
huge impact this librarian had on her friends. She wanted to make this same
kind of impact, but in a positive way. You get up in the morning and go to work

because you know you are going to make a difference in someone's life. It may be as simple and subtle as preparing a new book for the hold shelf or suggesting a title someone may enjoy, or helping someone sign on to the internet for the very first time or making a child laugh during story hour or perhaps even helping someone find a job. No matter the size of the task, you are making a difference to that individual person and, as a result, to your community as a whole. Let me repeat that: you are making a difference to the community as a whole.

However, when I peruse most library annual reports, I find cold, static numbers: circulation, gate counts, computer sessions, program hours, and attendance. These numbers are fine and important to track, but they do not go to the heart of the matter—that is, *your* heart. Circulation, gate count, and computer hours are not the reason you get up in the morning and go to work.

If these numbers do not get *you* excited, what makes you think your *community* will be any more excited? More to the point, if these static numbers do not motivate you as a librarian or a library staff member, how can you expect your library board, your city/county managers, and your community members to actively and excitedly support increased library funding?

The purpose-based library is not just about circulation, gate counts, and computer hours. It is about how you and your library impact people's lives and therefore the community as a whole. This is your most significant competitive advantage over the likes of Amazon, Google, and Netflix. In the next chapter we will examine the common mission of libraries and discuss how this mission can link to the reason you drive to work each morning.

POTTER'S PERSPECTIVE, POINTS, AND PONDERINGS

John brings up an important question for all of us. Why did we turn to librarianship as a career choice? For me, you might say it was "the family business." My mother was a volunteer school librarian at our elementary school in the early 1970s. She was high-school educated. My father was a maintenance pipefitter for Owens Corning Fiberglas. Both understood and appreciated the value of literacy and education. Due to my mom's volunteer work, I watched her select books in our family room. I watched her process books on our kitchen table. I spent several weeks helping her run inventory. This was one of my childhood experiences.

In 1976 I worked my first political campaign. My second cousin was running for magistrate judge. For many years, I walked neighborhoods, encouraged people to vote, and as a bonus saw many different ways of life. I also started to feel that there was something noble in working to make the world a better place.

After several more years and a fateful escape from a legal career path, I went to library school. In my first month I knew I had found where I belonged. I discovered that, for me, it was never about writing papers or doing research. What I loved about going to college was finding the answers for people. That is what I helped people do all day during my shifts on the reference desk at the University of Missouri. In my classes, we talked about the importance of free information and how the "people's university" can help break the cycle of poverty. I discovered the way that I could serve. Like lots of people, I went on a 20-year journey, only to wind up back where I had started.

What I have discovered is that a lot of the people who work in libraries have two common threads. First, they have a previous connection to other people who worked in a library. They understand that working in a library is a "people business." They understand that it is not about getting to read all day. They understand that it is work that connects people and resources. They also know about the warm feeling librarians receive from the work that we do. Second, they have a desire to make a difference in the world around them. This can take on several faces. Sometimes it is about helping people create businesses and stand on their own. Sometimes it is about helping children or adults learn to read. Sometimes it is about providing information on the topics of the day to inform the citizenry. These are still the reasons I'm excited to wake up every day and go to the library. I'd venture to say that you're the same way.

3
Missions, Visions, and Purpose

WHILE LIBRARIES EXIST TO TRANSFORM COMMUNITIES, THEY are on a path toward full automation, which will eliminate staffs' ability to have contact with their customers. In this chapter we identify a great paradox that lives within today's libraries. We propose that library staffs are too valuable of an asset to lose, for in our path to automation we lose the ability to (as Pikes Peak Library District likes to say) seek, engage, transform.

Before I visit a new client I like to familiarize myself with the organization's mission or vision statement. For example, the New York Public Library's (NYPL) mission statement reads:

> The mission of The New York Public Library is to inspire lifelong learning, advance knowledge, and strengthen our communities.[1]

As I reference above, my favorite of all time is from Pikes Peak Library District (PPLD):

> Provide resources and opportunities that change individual lives and build community. Seek, Engage, Transform.[2]

Seek, Engage, Transform. Wow. Simple and to the point, wonderful. However, in my work with libraries I often find a paradox. While the mission statement is inspiring, it does not often correlate with the primary services in which staffs actually spend their time. Rather than *Seek, Engage, Transform*, the default mission of the modern library appears to be to build a self-serve organization that is *Quicker, Faster, Better*. As you now know from the previous chapters, I play a major role in assisting libraries pursue *Quicker, Faster, Better*. I strongly believe for libraries to survive, this path is correct, as they must embrace the concepts of lean and become quicker, faster, better.

Therein lies the paradox. While you streamline your operations and you move to more digital interfaces and therefore reduce the face-to-face time you have with your customers, where does this wonderful mission statement of *Seek, Engage, Transform* truly fall in the future of libraries' priorities? How is your purpose fulfilled?

This paradox was clearly expressed at a meeting with the board members of one of my clients. The board was concerned about the amount of materials not being picked up from the holds shelf. I was asked to help the group examine and streamline their Holds Service Delivery Chain as well as evaluate the impact their lending policies had on their performance and cost. I began my presentation to the board by complimenting them on the library's holds/reserves system, which had a holds-to-circulation ratio of an impressive 30 percent (most of my client libraries fall into the 15-to-20-percent range). We presented our findings and recommendations on how to become quicker, faster, better as well as how to reduce the number of items left on the shelf (which turned out to be a high cost issue). At the end of the presentation the chairman of the board challenged the entire concept that a ratio of holds to circulation of 30 percent was a good thing. Her argument was that rather than just focus on a *Quicker, Faster, Better* holds and self-pick-up delivery system where customers are encouraged to not interact with the library staff, we should be restricting the level of books allowed for holds so we can increase the number of browsing customers. Well to say the least I was set back a bit, but there lies the paradox.

As stated in the previous chapter, to survive libraries must streamline their core operations, reduce clerical activities, increase self-service, embrace digital content and interfaces, and become quicker, faster, better. However, to go beyond survival, to succeed and grow, libraries must become much more than just self-service, efficient suppliers and distributors of books and media. They must embrace the purpose behind their mission statements. NYPL's mission is to inspire and strengthen their communities, and PPLD's mission is to build and transform. These are both good. I believe most libraries embrace and pursue a similar mission. *Quicker, Faster, Better* is only the price of admission for survival.

The title of this book is *The Purpose-Based Library*, not The Mission-Based Library. What is the difference between a mission and a purpose? A mission is a direction and path to guide, while a purpose is the passion that you have within. An organizational purpose is a passion you share with others in your organization. A mission can be cold and static, and a purpose is always warm and dynamic. A mission has a start and an ending, but a purpose has no beginning and no ending; it just is. A mission is something you are told to do, while a purpose is something that you can't help but do. A mission drives an organization on a determined path; a purpose drives itself. You as a member of your organization have within you a self-based purpose to help people. However, you are only one person and you can only do so much, but as an organization, where all of your passions are combined, a powerful compounding effect occurs. A purpose-based organization can transform entire communities. What a great reason to get up in the morning.

This common purpose is libraries' key to competitive differentiation with Google, Amazon, and Netflix. Figure 3.1 presents a new Venn diagram emphasizing the advantage libraries have.

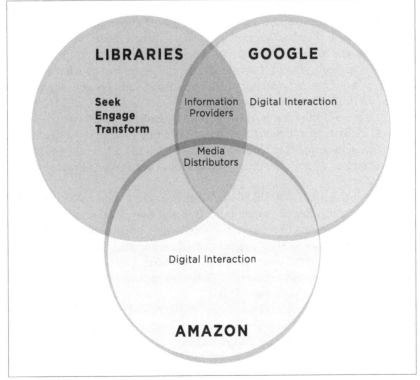

FIGURE 3.1
Competitive differentiation—libraries' advantage

One of my favorite things to do is ride along with the delivery driver as he runs his delivery route. I do this to get a full understanding of how a client's delivery system works. I have seen parts of North America that I never dreamed I would see. Some of the highlights include the day I spent with a Brooklyn Public Library driver, who while driving from branch to branch provided me a tour of New York that most New Yorkers never see. With the driver from the Okanogan (BC, CA) Regional Library I witnessed some of the most beautiful lake and valley scenery in the world. At Humboldt County Library we rode between the Pacific Ocean and the Redwood forests, in Western Maryland we crossed through the Cumberland Gap, in Tucson we traveled along the desert landscape, at Pikes Peak we rode with a mountain as our backdrop, in Pittsburgh we traveled through rolling hills atop the three rivers, and in Toronto I witnessed the vast diversity of the community the library supports. I could go on and on. What stays with me is the sheer number of communities that exist in the United States and Canada and the fact that there is a school and branch library present in every one.

As a longtime manufacturing consultant I always considered Walmart the most pervasive organization in the United States and, for that matter, the planet. After all, they have around 4,350 supercenters, clubs, or retail stores throughout the country.[3] Walmart also has a huge influence on US manufacturers' pricing policies and the products they offer, as well as what consumers buy. What other organization has a presence in nearly every community? You might think of the US Postal Service, which has around 31,500 locations[4] throughout the United States. However, this pales in comparison to the nearly 121,000 libraries[5] throughout the country. No one even comes close to the geographical coverage that libraries possess. Figure 3.2 shows the geographical penetration of public libraries.[6] Add in school libraries and the map would be florescent.

Each of these 121,000 US libraries has one common purpose behind its mission: to build a healthy community. It is a powerful statement. I propose that no other organization has more potential to impact the overall health and well-being of our nation's communities than libraries. So what is the most powerful and influential organization in the United States, Canada, and perhaps eventually the entire planet? The answer is libraries, and more to the point, a library with a purpose.

As a business consultant I assess the strengths and weaknesses of not only an individual organization, but also the overall group or industry they belong to. The geographical footprint libraries possess is one of the most important, powerful, and valuable strategic assets of any group, business, or industry I have ever come across. Add to the mix a highly educated workforce dedicated to serving the public, and you have the most valuable asset this nation possesses. We cannot allow this asset to be gutted, marginalized, or left to die a

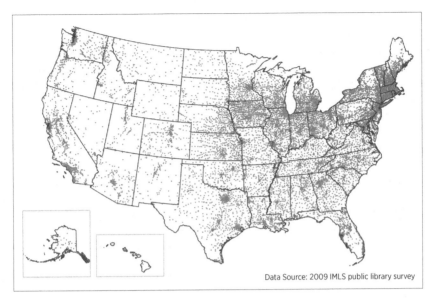

Data Source: 2009 IMLS public library survey

FIGURE 3.2
US public library locations

slow death. Libraries must leverage their geographical footprint, fully utilize their purpose-based staff, embrace their mission, and create a partnership with their community that will be of such value that libraries' path to success and growth is assured and celebrated.

Furthermore, we believe libraries are the right resource at the right time to recapture the purpose behind their mission and lead their communities toward a stronger, healthier state. Libraries are apolitical, they fight for the fairness of information access for all people, and most important, they are trusted. What other institution in today's broken society is better situated to make such a large impact in their local community?

POTTER'S PERSPECTIVE, POINTS, AND PONDERINGS

The most amazing talking point I was taught in library school is that there are more libraries in the United States than McDonald's restaurants—a staggering statistic that still holds true and one that should make libraries proud. Libraries should also be proud of our history when adopting new technology as a method of information access. I think it is surprising to people to learn how frequently libraries have been on the leading edge of technological adoption. Mid-Continent Public Library launched its first website in 1995, the same year that most of the world "discovered" the internet. The whole idea of ordering through an online catalog and picking up your order at a local store (sometimes called "bricks and clicks" or what Walmart calls "site to store") actually sounds a lot like interlibrary loan service and is something MCPL has been doing in some fashion since the early 1990s. Libraries are in every community both physically and in cyberspace and in greater numbers than any other institution. We are everywhere, but do we really take advantage of that fact? I would suggest that we do not.

Too often, libraries become a checkmark on a list of public assets that supposedly lead to a great quality of life. Do we have a park? Check. Do we have accredited schools? Check. Do we have a public library? Check. Is it good enough just to have a public library in your community, or should your public library be purpose based to truly earn that checkmark?

What is your library's purpose? Is it to check out books? Is it to be a jobs program? Is it to be publicly subsidized recreation for people who don't want to play sports? Is it to provide a spectacle so people can come and see what crazy thing is happening at the library this week? Many libraries seem to approach their work as though one of these services is their primary motive and therefore their purpose. We have to do better. Libraries are ideally positioned, both physically and virtually, to make a great impact on nearly every community in this country. The question is what does your community need and how can your library behave in a purposeful way to help achieve that community vision? We will address this key issue in the following chapters.

NOTES

1. "NYPL's Mission Statement," New York Public Library, www.nypl.org/help/about-nypl/mission.
2. "About the Library," Pikes Peak Public Library, http://ppld.org/about-the-library.
3. "Our Story," Walmart, http://corporate.walmart.com/our-story/our-business/locations.
4. "About," United States Postal Service, https://about.usps.com/who-we-are/postal-facts/size-scope.htm.
5. "Number of Libraries in the United States," American Library Association, last updated April 2014, www.ala.org/tools/libfactsheets/alalibraryfactsheet01.
6. "The Geography of US Public Libraries," Gothos, March 18, 2013, http://gothos.info/2013/03/the-geography-of-us-public-libraries.

4

The Community Pyramid

I N THIS CHAPTER WE SUBMIT THAT FOR A COMMUNITY TO BE transformed it must first understand its current state of health and wellbeing. To understand this you must not only define what this means, but you must also measure it. We propose that by defining your community's hierarchy of needs in the form of a pyramid you will better understand your community and the gaps and cracks that exist in your pyramid.

"What you measure drives performance, therefore, what you do not measure must not be important."[1] When I wrote those words a number of years ago, I was speaking primarily about customer service metrics. My point was, for example, if you do not know how long it takes to deliver a book to your customer then it must not be very important to you and your organization. These words also apply to the purpose-based library. To truly build and transform communities, your purpose must be more than a shared good feeling or a bunch of words printed on paper. Your purpose should be aspirational. You must define and measure what you wish to accomplish as a group because without definition, without measurements, it is an empty promise. Following that logic, we must define and measure your purpose and your mission.

Most everyone is familiar with Maslow's hierarchy of needs[2] shown in figure 4.1.

FIGURE 4.1
Maslow's hierarchy of needs

This pyramid represents a path to become a healthy, strong, and transformed human being. Maslow believed for humans to achieve the top level of the pyramid, namely self-actualization (one's full and creative potential), one must first satisfy his or her basic physiological and safety needs (food and shelter) and, once accomplished, one's psychological needs of belonging and self-esteem (relationships/accomplishments).

I have used the same approach to define the path for a healthy, strong, and transformed community. Figure 4.2 presents Huber's hierarchy of community needs.

Just like Maslow's hierarchy of needs, our communities strive for group self-fulfillment, specifically through the creative and philanthropic expression of their members. To reach this top level, the community must first satisfy the needs of every step of the pyramid. It must satisfy its foundational needs of food, shelter, safety, security, health, and nutrition. It must satisfy its basic needs of full functional literacy and digital literacy. It must satisfy its psychological needs of community engagement and contribution. Finally it must satisfy its long-term need of sustainability.

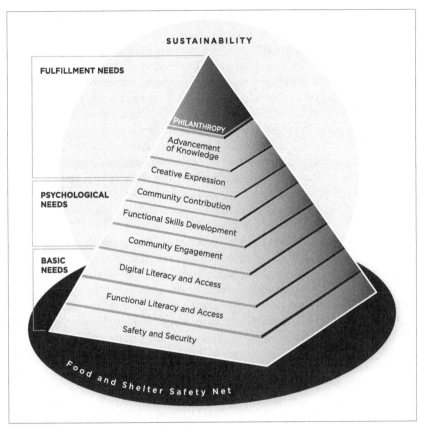

FIGURE 4.2
Huber's hierarchy of community needs

How healthy is your pyramid? Are there cracks in its foundation? Are there gaping holes preventing your community from climbing the steps? The purpose-based library would know the answers to these questions, because if you don't know, your library's mission and the purpose behind it are hollow, and you are telling everyone they are not important. To know the state of your pyramid, the purpose-based library must embark on specifically identifying the metrics that define your community's pyramid, create means to collect and monitor these metrics, and become the focal point or gathering place for the community to fix the gaps and holes in its foundation.

Libraries are already heavily engaged in each and every step of the community pyramid. Libraries offer resources for nutrition workshops, adult education, literacy, lifelong learning, writer's workshops, computer skills, jobs programs, homework assistance, government connections, and children's programs. However, if you ask the average person on the street what libraries do, you most likely will hear the response, "They lend books."

As president of a management-consulting firm, I know our services must first and foremost be a value-added resource. If my clients are to invest in our services, they must know that there will be more value created from these services than costs. We must present in concrete terms what specific improvements will be achieved and at what costs, otherwise our clients will see no value in our partnership. To accomplish this value analysis, we must understand how the system is performing in its current state and be capable of predicting how the system will perform in its streamlined lean state. Eventually we must measure the actual value-added impact to show the investment was sound.

Steve and I believe libraries are no different. They must be a value-added resource to their community beyond circulation numbers, gate counts, and program attendance. To fulfill the purpose and the mission, they must be able to present to the community the state of their pyramid, the gaps between where they are now and where they want to be, and how the library, along with the community, is closing these gaps. They must specifically present the metric value the library provides in their community partnership.

We define this metric-based role of the purpose-based library as the community steward, archivist, and town crier. Your library will become such an integral part of the community's path to improvement that it will be looked to first and foremost as the nonpartisan organization that brings together all the community players to repair the cracks and holes in the pyramid steps as well as to be the "keeper of the keys" for the progress made. Once a community recognizes the progress they are making because of their purpose-based library, funding will become a priority.

At this point you may be a bit overwhelmed by the vision we are presenting for the purpose-based library. If so, we would like you to take another moment and imagine tomorrow morning's drive to work. As you drive, you reflect on the 121,000 libraries in the United States and the 314 million people they serve. You realize this translates into only 2,600 people per library. You know that there is no other organization on the planet that has that kind of leverage. You know that you as an individual and you as part of your local community library make a difference every day to specific individuals, to your community, and to your nation as a whole. You understand that libraries and librarians are respected for being nonpartisan, neutral forces in today's divided and conflicted society. You remind yourself that if your library would simply embrace your common purpose by being a value-added community steward that defines, measures, and reports the health of your community pyramid as well as being a focal point for community resources, then your community would be transformed. You remind yourself that you are not alone—that there are 332,000 paid US library staff associates[3] plus countless volunteers who drive to work just like you do to pursue this common purpose. After all that is why you and they get up every morning.

In this chapter we presented Huber's hierarchy of community needs pyramid and the potential to define specific value-based metrics for each step. In chapters 6 through 16 we will further define the concept of these metrics and how they can represent a causal relationship between library services and community needs. However, before we dive into these metrics, we would first like to discuss what *community* really means in Huber's hierarchy of community needs, and we will do so in the next chapter.

POTTER'S PERSPECTIVE, POINTS, AND PONDERINGS

When John first proposed his hierarchy of community needs concept, it took some time to understand how different this paradigm might be for libraries. Honestly, libraries as a social service agency (helping those less fortunate and building to a higher purpose) seems pretty common to what we already do. Everyone knows that what libraries do, right?

Maybe not. In Mid-Continent's most recent strategic planning effort we invited one or two superintendents from the different communities to represent all the schools. We also invited one or two business advocacy groups and asked them to represent all businesses, along with other representatives for other communities within the library district. In total, we had between 15 and 20 people each time we convened a group. Most expected us to ask them what they wanted from the library. We didn't. Instead, we asked them to visualize the ideal community. They spent about an hour talking about the ideal community, and we listened. They talked about a lot of things, issues from financial literacy to aging in place to the plight of first-ring suburbs to homelessness to joblessness to philanthropy to opportunity. It was a wide-ranging and very stimulating conversation. After they started to gain consensus around the vision of the ideal community we then asked, "What can the library do to help fulfill that vision?"

This approach stunned our group. Several people told me that they had expected the session to take 30 minutes. MCPL would ask them what we needed to do, they would answer, "Buy more books," and we would be done. But two very important points came from the conversation. First, the participants told us that they got as much from the conversation as the library did. Many of them believed that the time spent would help them in their jobs. Bringing together people with different functions within the community exposed the whole group to new ideas, new trends and issues, and new struggles. Second, we began to see that a library with purpose would need to help address community needs to remain relevant. No more passive response. No more waiting for people to discover us. The purpose-based library had to be proactive.

I believe that when you build on a strong foundation, you can reach great heights. I also believe that the library may be ideally suited and in the best position to address a social problem that is at the foundation of your community. Sometimes this will come as a shock. Sometimes it will be obvious. But the key is that your community must stop thinking about the library as a place to borrow books. The library is an agent for great change and community betterment. Your library may be ideally suited to build the foundation for your community. This purpose is too important to leave to chance or to leave to the "the market." We have to plan, be deliberate, and be steadfast.

NOTES

1. John J. Huber, *Lean Library Management: Eleven Strategies for Reducing Cost and Improving Customer Services*, (New York: Neil Schuman, 2011) 41.
2. Abraham Maslow, "A Theory of Human Motivation," originally published in *Psychological Review* 50, no. 4 (1943): 370–96.
3. "Number Employed in Libraries," American Library Association, last updated April 2014, www.ala.org/tools/libfactsheets/alalibraryfactsheet02.

5

A Purpose-Based Community

I N THIS CHAPTER WE EXAMINE THE CONCEPT OF *COMMUNITY* IN Huber's hierarchy of community needs. We discuss the importance of a physical community and how your branch is perfectly positioned to become your community's transformational focal point.

I recently conducted a lean workshop for the Northeast Florida Library Information Network (NEFLIN). My wife and I stayed at Fernandina Beach located on Amelia Island, just north of Jacksonville, Florida. Amelia Island is about 13 miles long and two miles wide at its widest point and is defined by the Atlantic Ocean and the Intracoastal Waterway. The island's population is somewhat under 25,000 people. During my short visit, I was struck by the sense of community I found there. One person I met confirmed my thoughts by describing the island community as a modern Mayberry. (I even met their colorful version of Otis.) One night my wife and I visited a local tavern and witnessed firsthand this modern Mayberry. Children and dogs in tow, the young and old, the common and the eccentric embraced each other with hugs, dancing, and song all the while being entertained by musicians they call their own. As I sat on the deck I wondered how this sense of community had developed. Was it because they shared a common feeling of geographic separation from all other communities (even though they are only separated by a small bridge to the mainland)?

Times have changed, and for the rest of us, Mayberry only exists in reruns. Today communities are based on Facebook groups, the sports teams you follow, the church you attend, the clubs you belong to, and the hobbies you engage in but not the physical neighborhood you live in. We have defined our pyramid as the building blocks for a healthy and thriving community, but exactly what community are we representing, and does it really exist?

Over my 30 years of consulting, lean has taught me one overriding lesson: the larger an organization, the more complicated and harder it is to manage, measure, and transform; the smaller the organization, the simpler and easier it is to manage, measure, and transform. Over the last three decades, manu-facturing companies applied this lesson by reorganizing their large and mas-sive manufacturing plants into smaller plants and departments that focused on only a few products. They call them "focused factories." Cities and their communities are no different. To be effective in transforming a community, this community must be small and simple enough to be managed, measured, and transformed—in essence, a focused community. To successfully trans-form our pyramid, we must define it with this ground-level, focused commu-nity in mind.

School librarians know the names and faces of those children who strug-gle with early literacy, and they know the children who do not have access to the internet or a computer at home. Branch librarians know the names and faces of the moms who bring their children in each week, teens who come to the library for after-school programs, frequent readers who come in once or twice a week, the man seeking job assistance, and the homeless man looking for shelter. No one is closer to this ground-level, focused community than your school and branch library staff. Therefore, we propose to organize and define our focused community around the public schools and the branch library they feed. This also includes all the neighborhoods, businesses, and charitable orga-nizations that reside in this geographically defined branch community. For small cities with only one library, this is easy to define. Larger cities would be geographically divided into branch service zones, a task I would assume most libraries have already achieved.

However, geographically defining a community does not automatically create a Mayberry-like sense of community, especially if these community members are not even aware they have been defined as such. This sense of an Amelia Island community must be built, nurtured, and cared for. We believe the pyramid is the perfect vehicle for the library to accomplish this task. The purpose-based library and its pyramid would become the focal point for this transformation effort.

In the remaining chapters of this section, we address each step of the pyr-amid. As we climb each step, you will see how this sense of geographical com-munity can be built or reinforced. It will not happen in months and perhaps not in years, but we must remind ourselves that no one else has the kind of geographical footprint and leverage that libraries have. There is no other organization with people on the ground who are as well-educated and motivated to service their community as librarians and their staff. There is no other organization left that can organize an inclusive, focused, physical community around them. Therefore, we ask, if not libraries, then who?

POTTER'S PERSPECTIVE, POINTS, AND PONDERINGS

Mid-Continent Public Library is an independent political subdivision of the State of Missouri. Our service area includes three counties, 62 cities, 21 school districts, about 35 state House and Senate districts, and the divisions go on. Our district is 1,249 square miles and includes more than 776,000 people. It includes urban, suburban, exurban, and rural communities. Because we are independent, we try very hard to erase the political lines and just provide great library service. Sometimes that is easier said than done. Figure 5.1 shows the MCPL library district.

Previously, MCPL held a value of shared equality, as all of our libraries provided the same services; the only real difference was the size of the library.

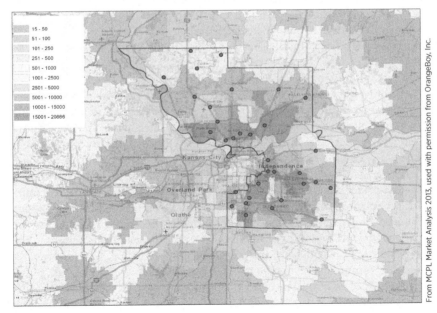

FIGURE 5.1
Mid-Continent Public Library district

From MCPL Market Analysis 2013, used with permission from OrangeBoy, Inc.

Think about a Starbucks. With the exception that some have a Clover brewer, there is no difference in the products and services they offer. If a particular area might warrant a larger Starbucks, they don't build a bigger one, they just build another one across the street or on the next block. MCPL shared that philosophy, and there were some benefits. It meant that our small rural libraries serving communities of fewer than 500 people had the same services as our libraries serving communities of 100,000 people. But that also led to some odd decisions. For instance, the deployment of the computer catalog was delayed for several years because data lines could not be run to our small rural communities. This held back our urban and suburban communities.

Another way to look at this is that the lowest common denominator ruled our decisions. Whatever everyone could agree to, everyone could have. For instance, each branch might have a teen advisory group. But given how different our communities are, we might not be able to universally offer everything the groups propose. So, the groups might become disillusioned because they would meet often but nothing would happen. Given the breadth of possibilities, and the less homogeneous our district became, the less reasonable it was to adhere to a policy of equality. Consequently, MCPL moved to a value of fairness.

Perhaps a better way to think about this is to consider what makes sense in a community. Does a community need a certain type of service? If so, then we can provide that service to that community. If others don't need the service, we don't have to employ it there. This may make sense, but it is risky. It may very well create differing levels of service in different locations. However, if we are deliberate about what we do, the services should be more in line with the expectations and desires of the community.

Libraries are more than buildings, they are service providers. Nearly every service organization I know tries to define their service area. If MCPL is going to erase political lines (except our own district lines, of course), how do we define our service areas? It takes a lot of work and effort, but over the past several years, we have been assigning US Census tracts to our branches to create service areas. Does that mean that a service area might cross a city or county line? It could, but that's not important. What matters is that we determine the general geography that corresponds with a physical library. That keeps our libraries from over serving some parts of our district while neglecting other parts. Figure 5.2 provides our Amelia Island type–focused communities, some served by multiple branches and some by a single branch.

The community pyramid provides us a further opportunity to focus, define, and understand the particular needs of our branch communities. One community may need more attention to children's literacy, while another may

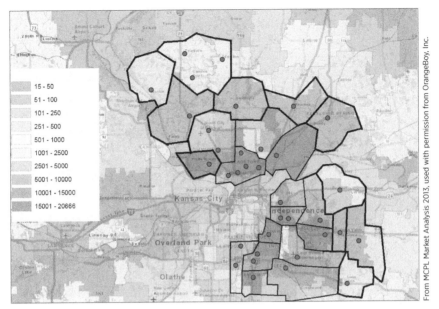

FIGURE 5.2
MCPL service areas, US Census tract

be simply struggling with community security. It provides an opportunity to expand our service model beyond books and computers to the unique needs the community pyramid expresses.

6
Dashboard Metrics

IN THIS CHAPTER WE PRESENT THE CONCEPT OF *DASHBOARD metrics*. We examine the successful characteristics of dashboard metrics and their importance to your community pyramid.

In chapter 4 we established that if a healthy and thriving community is important, and the hierarchy of community needs pyramid represents this community, then we must measure the health and well-being of this pyramid to confirm its importance. In chapter 5 we proposed that the branch library is the best means to define the community we wish to transform and the key to bringing all of this together is value-added metrics. As Steve and I researched the existing metrics available on the health of our national pyramid, we were struck by how ineffectual these metrics are for local communities. They are either outdated, complex, too high level to be useful, or not applicable. In this chapter, we introduce the concept of focused dashboard metrics and how these simple metrics can effectively define and measure the health and well-being of your local community pyramid.

Once again we would like to reengage you in your morning drive. While you drive, glance down at your dashboard. What do you see? In a brief second or two, you know your speed, your gas tank level, your battery charge, and if your oil pressure is safe. These metrics are visual, effective, and easily understood. For our community pyramid we also need metrics that can be understood at a glance. These simple and easy-to-understand metrics are called dashboard metrics.

Dashboard metrics have been a critical tool for the lean movement in the manufacturing industry. Hanging visible graphs and charts on the walls of a manufacturing plant is common; some have even installed electronic boards similar to sports stadium boards. More and more of my library clients are using dashboard metrics. For example, Frisco (TX) Public Library has a dashboard metric for "items returned to shelf within 24 hours." It hangs on the wall for all to see, and it shows in green the days they achieved 24-hour returns to shelf and in red the days they went over 24 hours. The group is very proud of their accomplishments and their dashboard metrics.

Another example of a dashboard metric all libraries can relate to is shelf accuracy. Figure 6.1 provides a dashboard that shows where you are now and how you have improved over time as well as metrics that reflect the cause and effect of the results. For example, the number of audits and hours of audits per quarter show a direct impact on shelf accuracy improvement.

For your community pyramid, dashboard metrics should meet the following criteria:

- easy to collect and analyze
- proactive rather than reactive
- visual
- simple and easily understood
- present relevant data for the local branch community's pyramid
- show a causal relationship
- provide a value perspective of the improvements
- driven in both a "top down" and "bottom up" direction

The last point of the criteria states the metrics should be top down/bottom up. The bottom-up metrics start at the local school library and the branch public library. The top-down metrics summarize these local community metrics to the city or county level as well as the state and national levels. The bottom-up metrics inform and inspire the coordination of local community members, including businesses, churches, neighborhoods, police precincts, and organizations. The top-down metrics inform and inspire the coordination of government and city leadership groups, including colleges, charitable organizations, corporations, and philanthropic resources.

For example, let us focus on the Functional Literacy and Access step of the pyramid. Assume there is a high rate of third-grade children in our local branch community who do not like to read and therefore are at risk of having poor literacy skills as adults. The local school librarian knows these at-risk children and coordinates with the local public library to create an after-school

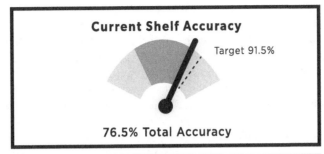

Current Shelf Accuracy

Target 91.5%

76.5% Total Accuracy

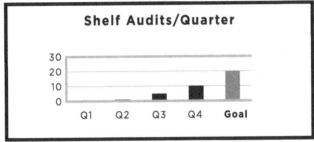

Shelf Audits/Quarter

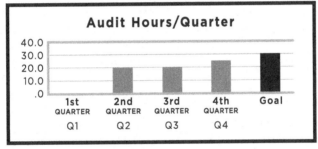

Audit Hours/Quarter

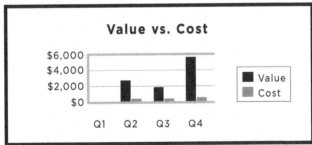

Value vs. Cost

FIGURE 6.1
Shelf accuracy

"love of reading" program to be hosted at the school by the library. The first place the library looks for assistance is not the city, state, or national government, but the local businesses, charitable groups, and volunteers. The library approaches these local resources and presents historical dashboard metrics on how the library's reading programs have impacted at-risk third graders' love of reading. The library shows national statistics on how eight percent[1] of these at-risk third graders will not graduate high school and 60 percent[2] will be incarcerated, as well as the national average cost of housing a prisoner in a minimum security prison at $18,476 per year[3] and the value of a high school diploma at $10,386 per year.[4] This is value-based bottom-up transformation.

However, assume that while businesses, charitable groups, and volunteers respond to these metrics by funding and volunteering resources, there are not enough library staff resources to coordinate, supervise, train, and support the after-school reading program. In addition, the program needs a van and a driver to take the children home after the program. By presenting specific metrics on how the after-school program has impacted the number of third graders who love to read, the community business leaders solicit city leaders to provide additional funds for library staff. The city responds by funding the program for this community as a pilot, while providing existing transportation resources to support the transportation requirements. The program is so successful that the city and a few philanthropic organizations provide funds to expand the concept to all the library communities by funding additional library staff, a dedicated van, and a part-time driver. This is top-down transformation. In addition, the state government sees the effectiveness of the program and funds a statewide initiative for after-school library reading programs for third graders. The success goes all the way to the national government, and federal funds are provided to libraries to assure rural communities can also benefit from library after-school "love of reading" programs. This again is top-town transformation. Transformation must come from the bottom and then, and only then, be supported by the top. Top-down transformation alone is ineffectual. For more information on top-down/bottom-up transformation refer to my book *Lean Library Management*.

While this example focuses on the literacy step of the pyramid, each library knows or will discover unique priorities for their community. One community may have already built a strong foundation for safe and secure neighborhoods; however, they may discover they have opportunities to improve their level of community engagement and participation. One community may first and foremost need to repair their adult literacy step prior to addressing higher-level steps. Some communities will be capable of addressing many steps at one time. Each community will decide where to focus their resources because they are closest to the issues and opportunities. Local libraries and their communities across the nation will become incubators for successful programs supported by bottom-up value-based metrics. Other libraries will adopt the most successful programs and then the nationwide top-down transformation will begin. The value of bottom-up and top-down transformation should be fully understood and embraced.

Some of the dashboard metrics you will see in the following chapters are easily collected or available from your current library's integrated library system (ILS). However, many of the metrics are a bit tougher. We look to five resources for help: research/reference librarians, businesses, charitable groups, community volunteers, and local newspapers. Research/reference librarians are highly skilled at researching and finding hard to come by data. The difference of course is that the data for a particular metric may not currently exist. Nonetheless, the skill set of a research/reference librarian should easily transfer to the management of dashboard metrics. The second and third resources are businesses and charitable resources. Businesses and charitable groups can be great resources to assist in the collection and presentation of this data. Also, many businesses host their own internal community events such as health and fitness programs. These businesses might be persuaded to extend some of their internal programs and tracking resources to the neighborhood community in which they belong. Fourth is the army of community volunteers, and finally and perhaps most important, local newspapers can be an invaluable resource for community information. Also, partnering with local newspapers in developing the dashboard metrics would create a great marketing opportunity.

We believe that when businesses and members of the local community understand the fractures in their local community pyramid, they will respond. Furthermore, we believe new avenues of funding will follow once these businesses and members of the community see firsthand the important value libraries provide in repairing these fractures. With these new avenues for funding, we believe the purpose-based library can move beyond a state of survival onto a path of success and growth.

At this point, you are probably thinking, "Our staff is already pressed to keep up with the day-to-day activities of running a library. How can we possibly engage in such a transformational effort?"

We offer the following thoughts to guide you in your strategic planning:

1. An Egyptian pyramid was not built in a day, nor will you define, measure, and transform your pyramid in a day. In fact, it took the Egyptians 20 years to build a pyramid. Imagine if your community could transform itself within a 20-year time frame. Would you deem that a major success?

2. Pyramids are built one block at a time. Your community can also be transformed one block at a time. You do not need to address the entire pyramid or even an entire step of the pyramid all at once.

3. You are already an expert. We believe there is no one else in the community that has a better feel for, or understanding of, the needs of your community than your library staff. You already know the priority needs of your community. Start on those blocks first.

4. Remember this is an entire community effort, not just a library effort.

5. Reimagine the skills your library staff will need to support this effort. Instead of book handlers, you will need facilitators and stewards. Instead of behind-the-desk reference librarians, you will need outreach librarians. Instead of research/reference librarians who deal with data already collected, you will need librarians who can research and develop new data about your community. In your future hiring decisions, consider these factors, and in your training programs, incorporate these new skills.

6. Be aware that a wealth of information for your dashboard metrics is available through the US Census Bureau, the Centers for Disease Control and Prevention (CDC), your local newspaper archives, and charitable and government agency reports.

7. Create simple dashboard metrics to begin with. If your library does not know, for example, the literacy rate of adults in your community, use national averages projected toward your community. This information is readily available. Also focus on what you do know. Librarians are great at counting. They count circulation, the number of people who enter their doors, hours of storytime, the number of new library cards, and so on. Create simple dashboard metrics by counting those things that directly impact your pyramid.

8. For data that is not available, encourage your research/reference librarians to build a support group through local business, school, volunteer, and university resources.

You are not alone. As the concepts in this book mature, library crowdsourcing surrounding the dashboard metrics will emerge and momentum will build. Plans are in place to develop a library support system based on this book's concepts. Go to www.purposebasedlibrary.com to get the latest news.

In the chapters to follow we present sample dashboard metrics for each step of the pyramid. These examples center around an imaginary community called the Oliver Underwood Regional Library (OUR Library). This imaginary community has 20,000 members, and most of its metrics presented reflect the national average of the topic at hand, such as homelessness or literacy, for example.

Finally, while it may seem overwhelming, libraries are well positioned to embrace the role of facilitator, archivist, and steward of your community transformation efforts. With a plan, a budget, retrained staff, and the resolve to make it happen, your library can transform your community. It is our objective to provide you a guide to help you in your efforts.

POTTER'S PERSPECTIVE, POINTS, AND PONDERINGS

In this chapter, we discuss a very important topic that is basic and essential but so often minimized and misunderstood. Many people no longer feel that the work that goes on at a library is important or necessary or even good. Some of this comes from the inherent distrust that people have of their government. It has become an article of faith among some that "the government" never creates anything. To overcome this worldview, we are challenged to prove that our efforts are effective, useful, and efficient. This is a challenge my mentors didn't face. It is no longer good enough to do good work. You have to prove that you're doing good work.

I started to see this transition when I was working on my master's in public administration. I routinely used Mid-Continent's annual report documents to discuss the topic of accountability with my class. These rather prescriptive documents did a very good job of telling people how the staff filled their days, weeks, months, and years. I just assumed that what the staff was doing was for the good. If we did more, that was obviously better.

Over the years, I began to challenge that notion, and more recently I did something revolutionary. I vowed to stop reporting the monthly circulation totals at our staff and board meetings. I've always believed that circulation is interesting and is a measure of general health. But it can also be misleading. I have frequently likened circulation to pulse rate. What if you take someone's pulse and it is 100? What does that mean? Is it good or bad? It could be bad if that person has been sitting in a chair watching television all day. On the other hand, it could be great if that person just finished running a 5K.

Suppose your library circulates 500,000 items. Is that good or bad? What does it tell us? Ok, let me give you more. Your library circulates 500,000 items and that represents an increase of three percent over the previous year. Economic factors may have had more impact on circulation than the great services we provide. Again, what does that mean? Think back to the question we asked our community focus group. Visualize the ideal community and consider what the library can do to meet that vision. How does circulating three percent more books this year over last year transform a community? Merely reporting what we did is no longer good enough.

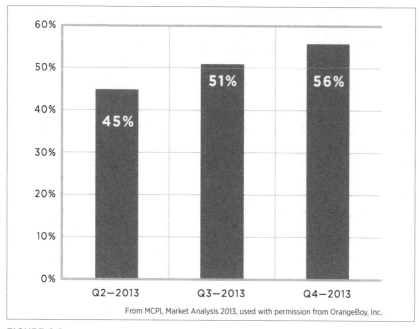

FIGURE 6.2
Market penetration

By contrast, what does figure 6.2 above tell you?

This graphic to me shows that market penetration is increasing each quarter. Market penetration in this context is a unique household with an active library card that has been used in the past 12 months. Is this more useful than broadcasting the per capita cardholder rate? You bet! Issuing cards is easy. Getting people to use the cards is what is hard. Market penetration shows that, and this metric is very, very easy to examine and determine if your library is making a difference.

Figure 6.3 shows a circulation metric presenting the number of items borrowed by different customer types. Early & Often users are adults who check out juvenile material. These are "storytime parents." Rising Stars are children who borrow children's materials. The chart suggests that MCPL's efforts to reach high-risk children and parents are working. It also underscores that parents and children in low-risk areas appear to be accessing the library in the highest numbers. Consequently, if the library wanted to focus on the moderate and high-risk areas with enhanced outreach efforts, it would be easy to justify and easy to visually demonstrate.

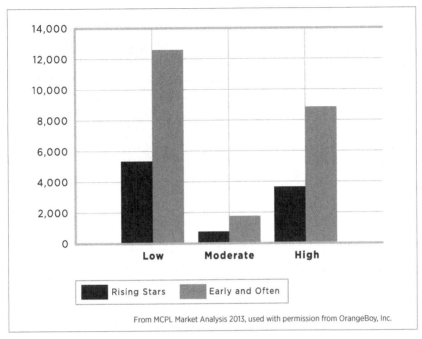

From MCPL Market Analysis 2013, used with permission from OrangeBoy, Inc.

FIGURE 6.3

Children's materials circulation by risk index

MCPL developed these dashboard metrics and market segments with considerable help from OrangeBoy, a "customer intelligence firm." With their guidance, MCPL created market segments to better address the needs of our community. OrangeBoy has helped us foster ongoing conversations with library users so we can serve everyone better. John and OrangeBoy share several clients, including the Kansas City Public Library, MCPL, and Tulsa City-County Library.

Our migration to reporting dashboards has required a lot of time and a lot of work with our partners. The key is aligning your dashboard metrics with the needs of your community and using these metrics to demonstrate real success.

NOTES

1. "High School Dropout Statistics," Statistics Brain, January 1, 2014, www .statisticbrain.com/high-school-dropout-statistics.

2. Ibid.

3. "The Price of Prisons: What Incarceration Costs Taxpayers—Oklahoma Fact Sheet" VERA Institute of Justice, January 2012, www.vera.org/files/price-of-prisons-oklahoma-fact-sheet.pdf.

4. Jason M. Breslow, "By the Numbers: Dropping Out of High School," WGBH, Frontline, September 21, 2012, www.pbs.org/wgbh/pages/frontline/education/dropout-nation/by-the-numbers-dropping-out-of-high-school.

7
The Food and Shelter Safety Net

IN THIS CHAPTER WE EXAMINE THE IMPORTANCE OF YOUR PYR-amid's safety net and the critical role your libraries can play in seeking out, engaging, and transforming the most vulnerable in your community. We present how simple dashboard metrics can shine a spotlight on the issue and how the library can be a focal point for tracking and presenting progress.

I recently attended an ILS user conference in San Francisco. The convention center sits at the dividing line between a wonderful downtown dining experience (on the right) and a disquieting, dangerous, and drug-infested downtown experience (on the left). We were advised therefore to always take a right when leaving the hotel entrance. On the first night my wife and I, having not yet received this advice and in a desire to buy groceries, took a left. After buying groceries, we exited the store, and a homeless man approached. I have traveled to many cities and have walked many urban streets at night. I have seen and encountered many homeless people. This was different. He had a swollen bloodshot right eye and heavy scrapes down the left side of his face. He wore a yellow tie, grey suit jacket, and torn, tattered pants and shoes. He said he was a businessman who had been mugged, his money and cell phone stolen. He of course was lying. Considering he looked rather dangerous, mentally deranged, and desperate, my first instinct was to ignore the man and protect my wife (and myself) by grabbing her arm and attempting to cross the street for the security of our hotel. I did just that, hoping to hear the chirping sound of the crosswalk. Unfortunately the only sound I heard (and felt) was a hard thunk on the back of my head. The homeless gentleman decided to reward me with a good thunking for ignoring him. During our entire trip we encountered surprisingly aggressive homeless people as they fought for attention. I heard similar stories from other conference attendees as well. When I shared this story with some San Francisco locals, they responded with laughter. We were guests in their community, and they responded by laughing. How healthy is San Francisco's pyramid?

A UNIQUE VANTAGE POINT

Downtown urban libraries are often within a short walking distance of homeless shelters. Many shelters close during the day, creating a large group of people seeking daytime shelter or a bathroom. Most libraries believe the homeless scare away downtown patrons from their library. From my personal observation, they have a point. I have witnessed various approaches to discourage "camping" at the library, including uncomfortable chairs, roving security guards, secured rooms, and rules for hygiene and behavior. Previously I asked how healthy San Francisco's pyramid was and implied that the community had simply accepted this homeless problem as a part of the permanent fabric of the community. However, I did find one part of the community trying to repair this fracture, the San Francisco Public Library (SFPL). In 2009, SFPL hired a social worker named Leah Esguerra, who launched a proactive homeless outreach program at their downtown library. The program was profiled in a story by local public radio station KALW: "Since the program's inception three years ago, Esguerra has reached out to nearly 1,200 homeless people at the library and referred them to city services. So far, 74 of them have also found housing."[1]

Many libraries have followed their lead, including my hometown library, the Tulsa City-County Library. Laurie Sundborg, former chief operating officer, explained the program:

> We partnered with the Family & Children's Services Homeless Outreach team based at the Salvation Army. We wrote several grants to fund a case manager for the library for 20 hours per week. He roams the building regularly interacting with customers. He connects people with various social services in the community to help with problems and as a result helps de-escalate confrontational situations, although we are clear that he does not serve as a security guard.

Public libraries are not the only resource available for those requiring a safety net. Many organizations exist to assist those at most risk in our community. For years I sat on the board of a wonderful charity in Tulsa called Neighbor for Neighbor (NFN). The organization provides free family counseling, bus fare, medical, dental, and vision care, and a discounted grocery store. Philanthropic members of the community such as the Kaiser Foundation, in combination with volunteer hours from doctors, dentists, and vision care professionals, support the organization. Other supporters include Catholic Charities, Mental Health Association, and John 3:16 Mission, as well as many other church organizations. As a board member I was surprised to find that many of these organizations work separately as opposed to hand in hand. I suppose it has to do with competition for limited funds. While at NFN I was also working on a project with the Tulsa City-County Library to improve their weeding program. It seemed a natural fit to have the library work through a cooperative program with NFN to distribute these weeded books to the poorest in the city. It was a great success and an example of cooperative community engagement.

Few organizations have the access and visibility to the homeless as a downtown urban library. Urban downtown libraries can therefore play a central role in helping charitable organizations work together to seek, engage, and transform the most vulnerable in our society. In addition, having the library as the central figure for these charitable groups eliminates the issue of competition. The library should work with these organizations to develop the community dashboard metrics. The purpose-based library would consolidate these metrics into one central community dashboard allowing the entire community to see and understand the impact and progress their community's effort has on helping the most vulnerable in our society.

THE CHANGING GEOGRAPHY OF POVERTY

In my discussions with Steve, he pointed out that poverty is just one unfortunate step from homelessness. He explained that while most believe homelessness is an urban issue it is becoming commonplace in suburbia.

In their groundbreaking book, *Confronting Suburban Poverty in America*, Elizabeth Kneebone and Alan Berube challenge many of the preconceived notions about poverty and even decouple the concepts of poverty and homelessness. In a recent presentation in Kansas City, Elizabeth Kneebone shared the following surprising information.

- As of 2002, more people live in poverty in the suburbs than in the urban core.

- Between 2000 and 2012, the suburban poor population increased in 93 of the top 95 metropolitan areas.
- By 2012, 59 of the top 95 metros found the majority of their region's poor located in the suburbs.
- In Greater Kansas City, over 30,000 more people live in the suburbs in poverty than live in the urban core.[2]

The conventional wisdom about poverty has consequences. In the urban core of Kansas City, there are scores of nonprofits addressing poverty and homelessness. Meanwhile, poverty and homelessness are growing in the suburbs and relatively few resources or organizations are focused on these problems. In terms of resources, the average poor urban resident has $3,419 of resources allocated compared to $857 for poor suburbanites. Kansas City has terrible mass transit. Consequently, 27 percent of low-income urban dwelling people have access to public-transit-accessible jobs, while only 12 percent of their

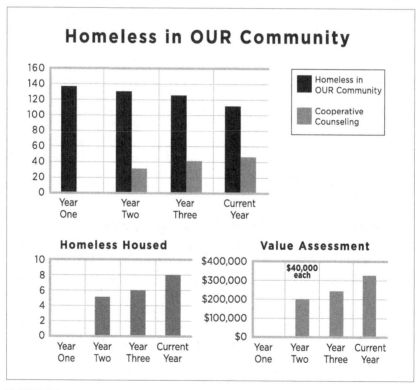

FIGURE 7.1
Homeless impact

suburban counterparts have similar access. Free and reduced lunch program participation is increasing in the suburbs.[3] A major demographic shift is under way. Poverty is no longer an exclusively urban issue.

Figure 7.1 presents our example dashboard metric for homeless in OUR Library community. In this dashboard and many more to follow, we provide a value assessment of the cause-and-effect improvement of the community's efforts. In this case we base our cost of homelessness from a 2012 statement by HUD Secretary Shaun Donovan that "it costs the public $40,000 for a homeless person to be on the streets because of the expenses of emergency room visits, jail time and hospital stays."[4]

Once again, you should focus on those issues that most impact your community. It may be homelessness, or it may be hunger. Your community library working with your community members should define your community priorities. Your research/reference librarians should develop their own local assessment of the cost of homelessness or value of food programs or simply use averages from a national perspective.

POTTER'S PERSPECTIVE, POINTS, AND PONDERINGS

There are several things that libraries can do to help contribute to the social safety net around hunger issues. For example, Mid-Continent Public Library has taken on food drive challenges periodically. But most of the time these efforts have not been aligned with our goals or our larger community strategy. Don't get me wrong. The local food pantries always appreciate our efforts. But what if we were more deliberate?

Any time you try to help someone, it is important to learn the best way to help. Over the years, the message I've received is that, while food collections around Thanksgiving and Christmas are nice, it is the summer that becomes the season of greatest need. Children aren't in school and don't have access to the free and reduced breakfast and lunch programs. While our hearts are full of generosity during the holiday seasons, frequently food donated in November won't last until July or August.

We started a "food for fines" program that correlated with our summer reading program (SRP). The idea was to encourage people to clean up accounts so children can more easily participate in SRP. We allowed people in the community to donate food to pay off someone else's fines. This program was a win-win-win. Library accounts became clear so that children could read in the summer. Food pantries were stocked in the time of greatest need. People in need had access to community safety net resources.

Don't misunderstand the point of the chapter. If your library attempts to directly address the hunger and homeless problem in your community, you will likely be accused of "mission creep," and I think I would agree. However, you can be more proactive. You can help by coordinating and cooperating with other agencies and by providing information and dashboard metrics to the larger community about the issue. Independence, Missouri, has created a Hunger and Homeless Coalition similar to the concept presented in this chapter. The mission of the coalition is for all service providers to be able to share information with each other and within the community regarding services they offer and community needs that have been assessed. Currently MCPL is not part of this coalition. We believe by joining this coalition and taking on the responsibility to track and display these dashboard metrics in our community library as well as our annual report, we can lead the community to increased involvement, better solutions, and better results.

In communities where you have a cooperative effort, find how you can help. For communities that do not have a cooperative effort, become the focal point in creating such a coalition as well as being the resource to manage the dashboard metrics.

NOTES

1. Julia Scott, "Helping the Homeless at the S.F. Public Library," KALW Local Public Radio, January 18, 2012, http://kalw.org/post/helping-homeless-sf-public-library.
2. Elizabeth Kneebone, "Confronting Suburban Poverty in Metropolitan Kansas City," Brookings Institute, June 2014, www.marc.org/Community/First-Suburbs-Coalition/Assets/ConfrontingSuburbanPoverty_June2014.aspx.
3. Ibid.
4. Molly Moorhead, "HUD Secretary Says a Homeless Person Costs Taxpayers $40,000 a Year," PolitiFact.com, March 12, 2012, www.politifact.com/truth-o-meter/statements/2012/mar/12/shaun-donovan/hud-secretary-says-homeless-person-costs-taxpayers.

8
Safety and Security

I N THIS CHAPTER WE DISCUSS THE IMPORTANCE OF THE PYRA-
mid's foundational step: Safety and Security. We propose that libraries can
play a key role in providing resources and coordinating volunteers to impact
the safety and security of your community. You will discover simple dashboard
metrics to track and highlight your community's progress.

A CBS *60 Minutes* segment called "Counterinsurgency Cops: Military
Tactics Fight Street Crime" aired in August of 2013. The title of the segment
presents a rather scary image; however, as the segment unfolds it provides a
totally different picture. The story is really about the power of organizing a
local community. Mike Cutone served as a Green Beret in Iraq prior to becoming a police officer. While serving, Mike learned that to make a community
safe you must have the trust, cooperation, and involvement of the locals. After
his service, Mike became a Massachusetts state trooper and transferred his
experience to a crime-ridden area in Springfield. In the report Mike states,
"Insurgents and gang members both want to operate in a failed area, a failed
community, or a failed state. They know they can live off the passive support
of the community, where the community is not going to call or engage the
local police."[1] In one scene the community police, local businesses, and community members meet to discuss the progress they have made. While I do

not know where they were meeting, I imagined it was their local community library.

The lesson Mike teaches us is that your local pyramid cannot be healthy unless the community is involved and bound together for secure and safe neighborhoods. The National Crime Prevention Council (the one with the dog McGruff as their spokesman) appears to agree. It recommends joining or forming a neighborhood watch program:. "Neighborhood Watch is one of the oldest and most effective crime prevention programs in the country, bringing citizens together with law enforcement to deter crime and make communities safer."[2] As we have established, there is no other organization with a larger geographical footprint than the library system. School and public libraries have the ability to organize, communicate, and educate as well as provide meeting spaces. While at first it might sound strange, it is a natural fit for the library, and it provides the first opportunity to form your geographically based communities around your branch library.

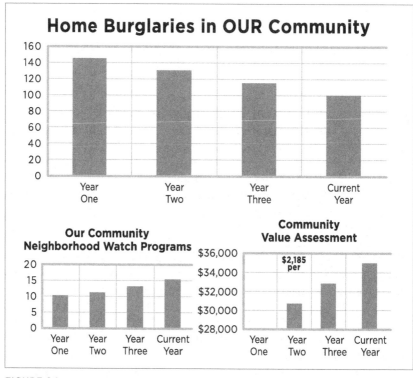

FIGURE 8.1
Safety and security

A great tool to begin this process is Nextdoor.com. It basically is a neighborhood "facebook." I recently became the communications director for our neighborhood, and I am using this tool to create a sense of common interests for my neighbors. It allows neighbors to share alerts including, for example, strange vehicles, lost dogs, break-ins, property damage, lost UPS packages, and contractor reviews. By using Nextdoor.com and tools like it, libraries can be seen as a focal point for community organization, the first step toward creating your Amelia Island. A failed community that has given into crime will never have a pyramid to climb. The purpose-based library can make a difference by bringing neighborhoods and communities together to understand and respond to the safety issues they must overcome.

Figure 8.1 provides a proposed dashboard for your pyramid.

There are many other metrics you may choose, such as domestic violence, incarcerations, and juvenile detentions. Your local community and local police should decide which metrics will have the biggest impact. For information on your community, refer to the CrimeReports website at www.crimereports.com. Working with the police, your library can use these metrics to raise public awareness and focus resources on the areas of greatest need.

POTTER'S PERSPECTIVE, POINTS, AND PONDERINGS

I am often surprised by the community's perceptions about libraries and safety. Over the past several years we have had our share of break-ins, copper theft, and even a few cases of assault. I tend to believe that the violence that surrounds our libraries, from time to time, spills onto our property. What has surprised me is when people don't expect us to be upset by theft and violence in our neighborhood. In fact, I'll never forget one person telling me that he was shocked that I was looking to press charges on a copper thief. He suspected that the library would look the other way in an attempt to decrease the number of reported crimes in the neighborhood. As John says, "If you don't measure it, it is not important."

People can't build community if they don't feel safe and secure. The first neighborhood watch program in Independence was formed in 1996 by Jan Jordan, a mother of four daughters who heard of a prowler in her neighborhood. She became concerned for the safety of her family and took it upon herself to organize her neighborhood into a "watch area."[3] Jan has remained a driving force behind the neighborhood watch program, helped to organize three separate watch groups over the years, and organized and kept track of each of the watch groups throughout the city. Currently, there are more than 50 registered watch groups in Independence, and these numbers are rising.

We have to position ourselves to make our community better. Instead of waiting for people like Jan to act, what if the library made a commitment to have a community open house once a year? We could invite all sorts of social services and public safety resources to the event and hear the concerns of the community. If there is an issue around safety and security, we can help provide a community response.

The question we must ask ourselves is, if the public library system had become an additional resource for people like Jan in 1996, how many crimes could have been prevented and how much safer would our neighborhoods be? Let us not wait another decade or two to ask the same question again.

NOTES

1. "Counterinsurgency Cops: Military Tactics Fight Street Crime," *60 Minutes* video, 13:17, August 4, 2013, www.cbsnews.com/news/ counterinsurgency-cops-military-tactics-fight-street-crime-04-08-2013.
2. Jason Wilkens, "Neighborhood Watch," National Crime Prevention Council, April 16, 2009, www.ncpc.org/topics/home-and-neighborhood-safety/ neighborhood-watch.
3. "History," City of Independence, Missouri, website, www.ci.independence .mo.us/NeighborhoodWatch/History.aspx.

9
Health and Nutrition

IN THIS CHAPTER WE DISCUSS THE IMPORTANCE OF THE NEXT foundational step of your pyramid and how your library can play a proactive role in affecting your community's overall health and nutrition. We present how simple dashboard metrics can track your community's progress and highlight the role your library plays.

For many communities, the Health and Nutrition step of the pyramid is severely fractured. Once again, libraries have the ability to coordinate the resources and information to improve their local communities' health. I only have to look down Route 66 for an example.

In 2008, Oklahoma City Mayor Mick Cornett challenged his city to lose one million pounds. The challenge included an educational web page on health topics, corporate sponsors, success stories, community groups, organized fun runs, and resource links as well as a site for neighborhood organizers.

In January 2012, Oklahoma City hit the one million pound goal, and the foundation of the program was centered on neighborhood groups. From their website:

> Joining a Neighborhood group is easy. Just sign in to the web site and
> "Join a Group." If you see your Neighborhood, click to join it. If you don't

see your Neighborhood, you can ask that it be created. By forming and joining a Neighborhood Group, your Neighborhood will be recognized on the web site and the members of the Neighborhood Group can see stats about their neighborhood. Get Healthy, Lose some Weight, and Take a Walk—We can do it, together in our Neighborhoods.[1]

During my time as a Neighbor for Neighbor board member, nutrition was an important topic. The doctors on our board explained that the number one issue the poor face is poor nutrition combined with poor fitness, which often leads to diabetes. Libraries have a wealth of information on health and nutrition just waiting for people to come in and read. Libraries must no longer wait until those in need walk through the door—they must be proactive by *seeking, engaging, transforming.*

When I was in the fifth grade, my neighborhood participated in a Fourth of July parade. All the neighborhood kids decorated wagons, and we marched down the street waving our American flags. It is a great memory. I believe our elementary school organized it. It involved about five different neighborhoods, and it was a great time for my friends and me. Simpler times perhaps, but school and public libraries should be a focal point for communities to come together. Libraries can impact this step of the pyramid by establishing local fun runs, parades, health and nutrition fairs, and many other events limited only by your imagination. By doing so you continue to build upon the sense of community we strive for with the branch library as a focal point. If libraries create the opportunity, we are convinced local community leaders will naturally rise from the neighborhoods to lead these efforts.

In figure 9.1 we present our example health and nutrition dashboard for OUR Library community. In OUR example we use the national average of 1.9 million newly diagnosed cases of diabetes in 2010[2] against OUR population of 20,000. We base our valuation of the reduction in newly diagnosed diabetes cases in OUR community on this American Diabetes Association statement: "The total estimated cost of diagnosed diabetes in 2012 is $245 billion, including $176 billion in direct medical costs and $69 billion in reduced productivity."[3]

The above dashboard and those to follow use national statistics. Your library will use more targeted data reflecting your own community's experience. For example, the website www.usdiabetesindex.com tracks the diabetes index and promises a wealth of data. It does require a subscription, however. From the website:

The U.S. Diabetes Index (USDI) is a "power-tool" that provides the most comprehensive source of available data about diabetics, their care, and the trends that are shaping the U.S. diabetes market. It contains more than 30,000 tables, maps, charts and graphs by nation, state, county,

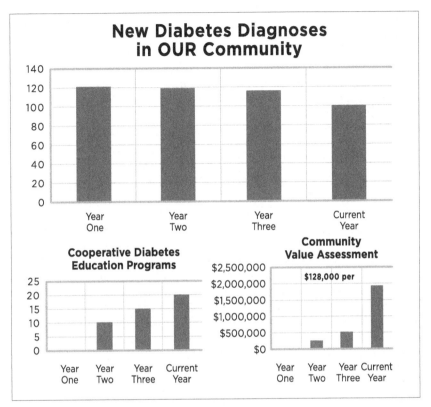

FIGURE 9.1
Health and nutrition

city, congressional district, state legislative district, and zip code. USDI
further segments diabetes data by race/ethnicity, age, and gender.[4]

POTTER'S PERSPECTIVE, POINTS, AND PONDERINGS

John and I keep discovering that we have more in common every time we
talk. We live in cities where ice storms and tornados are common. But one
additional common characteristic, which shouldn't be a point of pride, is that
both our hometowns are listed among the fattest cities in the United States.
In fact, a *Men's Fitness* report named Tulsa number 11 on the list and Kansas
City number 22.[5]

Libraries need to help address community health, and I believe we need
to start by setting a good example and lead the way by undertaking health and

wellness programs for their employees. These programs need to be strategic. Programs that buy gym or Weight Watchers memberships for everyone frequently fail. We have been successful by employing a wellness coach through our insurance company. She has been very good in helping us make changes in our culture. Not long ago we had a building-wide luncheon at our administrative headquarters. Without prompting, our staff members selected a menu made from very healthy choices.

I'm not exactly sure when this happened, but in America the unwritten rules for morning meeting food dictate muffins or doughnuts. We stopped doing that. I keep a basket of snacks on my office conference table. The basket contains dried fruit, trail mix, nuts, protein bars, and sugar-free candies. If I want to be serious about my community's health, I have to start in my office.

We also worked with our insurance broker to take advantage of a program called "cost-plus." It is a form of self-insurance that rewards us for positive health decisions. In recent years, our loss ratio has been very favorable.

Our employees think about health and wellness. This has resulted in some interesting program offerings. For many years, MCPL has offered flu shots in our libraries. We started before the advent of the pharmacy-based clinics. In fact, for several years in the early 2000s, MCPL was responsible for distributing more Red Cross flu shots than any other location in Greater Kansas City. With flu shots more easily available, we have scaled back on these offerings. However, we still do this, especially in our small, rural communities where health care is not as easily available.

More recently, we have ventured into more physical programs like art walks and even Tai Chi classes for our public. This year we decided to really try something different by providing an online health guide for our public. *Gym-America* is a custom diet planner and fitness tracker that allows you to create exercise and diet plans based on your individual needs, goals, and schedules. It includes hundreds of instructional workout videos, recipes, and other tools to help you meet individual fitness goals. With an MCPL card, anyone can set up an account and start working on individual fitness.

Our pyramid metrics tell us that health and fitness should be a priority for our community, and therefore it should be a priority for our library system. These metrics can be very effective in raising public awareness as well as supporting our marketing efforts. We plan to continue our internal focus on health and fitness which will help us be better prepared to align our strategic efforts for our most in-need branch communities.

NOTES

1. "Neighborhoods," OKC Million, www.thiscityisgoingonadiet.com/about/neighborhoods.

2. "2014 National Diabetes Statistics Report," Centers for Disease Control and Prevention, www.cdc.gov/diabetes/pubs/estimates11.htm.

3. "The Cost of Diabetes." American Diabetes Association, last updated April 18, 2014, www.diabetes.org/advocacy/news-events/cost-of-diabetes.html.

4. U.S. Diabetes Index website, www.usdiabetesindex.com.

5. Nate Millado and Sara Vigneri, "The Fittest and Fattest Cities in America," *Men's Fitness*, www.mensfitness.com/weight-loss/burn-fat-fast/the-fittest -and-fattest-cities-in-america.

10
Functional Literacy and Access

IN THIS CHAPTER WE EXAMINE WHY, DESPITE THE EFFORTS OF schools and libraries, illiteracy remains a chronic problem for communities and prevents many in our communities from climbing higher on the pyramid. We propose that your library can play a more proactive role in coordinating the resources of your community to positively impact this trend. We present simple dashboard metrics that will highlight your library's impact on your community's literacy rates.

In previous chapters we addressed the pyramid's Food and Shelter Safety Net as well as the foundational steps of Safety and Security and Health and Nutrition. Climbing up our pyramid we find next the foundational step of Functional Literacy and Access, to which libraries are already heavily committed. This step of the pyramid has three segments: preschool, student, and adult functional literacy. In the following sections, we will define what literacy is, assess the current literacy gap, and propose dashboard metrics for each of these categories.

PRESCHOOL LITERACY

For our pre-K definition of literacy we look to Multnomah County (OR) Library for inspiration. From their website:

> Young children need a variety of skills to become successful readers. A panel of reading experts has determined that six specific early literacy skills become the building blocks for later reading and writing. Research indicates that children who enter school with more of these skills are better able to benefit from the reading instruction they receive when they arrive at school.[1]

Using Multnomah County's list of skill requirements for early literacy, we developed this synopsis for defining pre-K literacy skills:

Vocabulary Motivation. Able to identify and recite the names of things

Print Motivation. Enjoys being read to, likes playing with books, pretends to read, and looks forward to a trip to the library

Print Awareness. Understands the flow of words on a page as they are being read (left to right, top to bottom)

Narrative Skills. Capable of listening to a storybook and verbally retelling the story to the storyteller

Letter Knowledge. Capable of recognizing, verbalizing, and writing letters in the alphabet

Phonological Awareness. Ability to hear and create rhymes, say part of words as sounds, and put parts of word sounds together

According to the National Institute of Early Education Research (NIEER), preschool in America is in a state of emergency:

> Adjusted for inflation, state pre-K funding fell $550 million. This decrease amounts to nearly $450 per child. Real spending per child is now at its lowest level since we began our survey in 2002, $1,000 below its level a decade ago. This bad news on funding was widespread. State pre-K spending per child declined in 27 of 40 states with programs. In 13 states spending per child fell by 10 percent or more from the previous year. Only 12 states and the District of Columbia increased spending per child in 2012.[2]

The American Association of School Librarians research article, "Preschool Education through Public Libraries," provides us the following guidelines:

> 1. Children's early experiences with children's books are among the most significant correlates with their success in learning to read in school. Specific aspects of these books, such as the interest level

for children and ease of understanding and remembering the story, make the experience even more effective (Mason and Kerr 1992; Morrow 1993).

2. Children are more motivated to request being read to, and to "read" or explore on their own, from books with which they are already familiar or have heard or read before and have enjoyed (Brock and Dodd 1994; Dickinson et al. 1992; Herb 1987; Schickedanz 1993).

3. There is a positive relationship between how much children have been read to and how well they will read (Lancy 1994; Scarborough, Dobrich, and Hager 1991; Wells 1985).

4. Storybook reading is a more effective influence on literacy development when children have opportunities to engage in conversation about the story (Mason and Kerr 1992; Norman-Jackson 1982; Pellegrini and Galda 1994).[3]

Kathleen McCartney, PhD, dean of Harvard Graduate School of Education, states that children gain a lot from going to preschool: "At preschool, they become exposed to numbers, letters, and shapes. And, more important, they learn how to socialize—get along with other children, share, contribute to circle time."[4] NIEER estimates that in 2005 two-thirds of four-year-olds and more than 40 percent of three-year-olds were enrolled in a preschool education program.[5] Need we remind ourselves, a parent reading to their child is the first and most important step in developing a child's basic reading skills? According to a Reading Is Fundamental survey conducted in June 2013:

- 50 percent of parents say their children spend more time with TV or video games than with books.
- 87 percent of parents say they currently read bedtime stories with their children on average five times a week.
- Printed books are the format of choice for 76 percent of parents of children age eight and younger.
- Twice as many children prefer a printed book (20 percent) over an e-book (9 percent), say parents who read both types of books to their children.
- 55 percent of parents reported impediments to reading with their children, with the most common being not enough time in the day (35 percent), child not interested (14 percent), not enough money to buy books (7 percent), limited access to library (4 percent), parent not interested (2 percent), and other reasons (5 percent).[6]

As encouraging as it is to see that 87 percent of parents read to their children on average five days a week, for our healthy pyramid we need that other 13 percent to be healthy readers as well. Is it not curious that our adult illiteracy

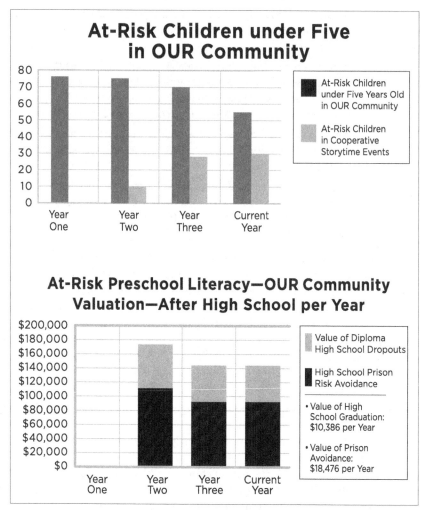

FIGURE 10.1
Preschool literacy

rate is 14 percent, 13 percent of our parents do not read to their children, and 14 percent of children are not interested in being read to? The issues of a child showing no interest, not enough parent time to read, and not enough money to buy books are areas where the community can help, specifically the school and public libraries.

Identifying at-risk children in a community is the key challenge. School librarians in conjunction with the kindergarten teachers know which children and which families face the biggest challenges in preparing their children for school. These children may have a brother or sister at home under the age of five. School librarians can seek and engage these families and help them connect with public library resources or other community resources such as Head Start. In addition, public libraries can seek and engage current patrons for assistance in recruiting potential at-risk children for their storytime programs. To create OUR dashboard metrics, we turn to the US Census Bureau. For OUR imaginary community we use the national average of the number of children under the age of five with a working mother and no child-care arrangements as 1.2 million, or 10 percent of all preschool candidates.[7] In addition, we used the national average of the number of third graders who will eventually not graduate from high school (8.1 percent)[8] and the percent of high school dropouts who will eventually end up in jail (60 percent).[9] We support OUR valuation of reducing this number on the national average cost of housing a prisoner in a minimum-security prison at $18,476 per year[10] and the value of a high school diploma of $10,386 per year.[11] See figure 10.1.

Other groups in your community are also focused on early child education and can be a resource for additional dashboard metrics. NIEER estimates 40 percent of all children are in some kind of Head Start, state sponsored, or special education program.[12] For example, the Tulsa-based Community Action Project (CAP), considered a model for the nation, assists low-income families with early childhood development programs. They were featured on a national CBS news broadcast on May 4, 2013.[13] Table 10.1 presents an example of CAP's dashboard metric from their annual report.[14] By contacting and coordinating resources with all the pre-K programs in your community you can expand the depth of your community dashboard and your effectiveness in identifying at-risk children.

TABLE 10.1

CAP enrollment

Total Funded Enrollment	
Early Head Start	260
Head Start	1,351

Percent of Eligible Population Served through Funded Slots	
Early Head Start	5.43%
Head Start	29.09%

POTTER'S PERSPECTIVE, POINTS, AND PONDERINGS— PRESCHOOL LITERACY

When Mid-Continent Public Library worked with OrangeBoy to set up our market segmentation, an interesting question was posed to the senior leadership team. What is our number-one goal? If we had to start shedding the things we do, what is the one thing that we do where we are best positioned to make the greatest impact? This was a great question and sort of like asking your grandmother who is her favorite grandchild. However, without missing a beat I said, "early childhood literacy." Why was this so obvious to me?

Much of my response was based on what we've been talking about in the previous chapters. Libraries have a great physical footprint. Libraries have a very low threshold to entry. Libraries are egalitarian, allowing all to enter regardless of income, social status, or other potential barriers. Libraries have market recognition around early childhood literacy. While we struggle for people to associate the public library as a place to get digital books, most people know libraries conduct preschool storytimes. Early childhood literacy work meets an expectation and lines up with a positive stereotype. But what is that stereotype? Do people think we facilitate playdates, or do they understand that we actually are supporting school readiness? Do they understand that the finger plays and stories are actually building the foundation for the child's (and the community's) long-term success?

At MCPL we started to think very seriously about early literacy. Sly James, the mayor of Kansas City, shared an idea with me shortly after he took office. He believed that Kansas City should set a goal to attain grade-level reading throughout the city by third grade. I thought that was very ambitious. He created an initiative called Turn the Page KC, and we were invited to the various meetings. Very early on, we held up our summer reading program as a means to help meet this goal. Almost immediately, I saw a problem. While everyone acknowledged that summer reading was a good thing, there was very little research supporting the hypothesis. Along the same lines, I wasn't finding much that I could stake the effectiveness of our program on. Was our program making a difference? I knew that more children participated each year, but that wasn't satisfying.

Eventually, we started to work on a very simple project. With the help of the Kansas City Area Education Research Consortium, we did a test-incident-posttest study. The consortium accessed the standardized reading metrics from the schools for children in the spring, matched them with library summer reading participation, and then matched them again with the reading scores the following fall. The library was shielded from the student's personal information. The schools were shielded from the student's library activity. In the end, we discovered not only that our free summer reading program combats summer slide (a student's loss of knowledge over the summer), but also that children who participated in the summer reading program actually scored higher on their tests in the fall. What is more important, if they participated in our summer reading program, students with high-risk characteristics or attending lower performing schools actually scored higher on their fall test scores. Summer reading can help children catch up if they are behind. We can now prove it and present it in our dashboard metrics.

Wouldn't your local school board like to know this? How valuable will your library be in your community if you can prove that you effectively prepare children for school success and that you can help remediate those that need help *and* that you can do so before that critical third-grade benchmark?

STUDENT LITERACY (THIRD TO FIFTH GRADE)

The literacy rates among fourth-grade students in America are concerning. In 2013 more than 66 percent of all US fourth graders scored "below proficient" on the National Assessment of Education Progress (NAEP) reading test, meaning they were not reading at grade level. Among these low-performing fourth-grade students, 80 percent came from low-income families.[15]

Reading proficiency among middle school students isn't much better. On the 2013 NAEP reading test, about 22 percent of eighth graders scored below the "basic" level, and only 36 percent of eighth graders were at or above grade level.[16]

While the data presented above is useful and gives us a ballpark measuring stick, it does not meet our dashboard metric criteria. The larger the group, the blurrier the problem, and as a result the more off-target the solution. The people who really know the functional literacy rate of their community are the local school librarians and the local branch staff. This is where we must focus our dashboard metrics.

To establish our dashboard metrics we must first have a common definition of *literacy*. We chose Scholastic's four categories of skills for our definition of *student literacy* (third through fifth grade).[17] We summarize it as follows:

Fluency. Recognize words and quickly and accurately read out loud with expression.

Comprehension. Able to articulate the main idea of a story, place events in sequence, and summarize the story orally or in writing.

Spelling and writing. Able to use a dictionary to look up words not known, research and compose a simple report from a variety of sources, and revise compositions with help of a teacher.

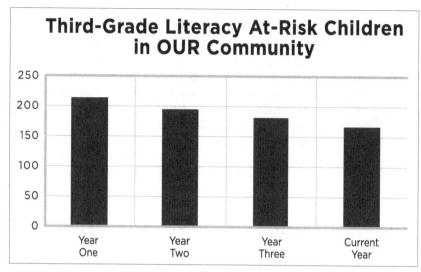

FIGURE 10.2
Third-grade literacy

Vocabulary. Able to figure out word meanings from clues in the text, use synonyms and antonyms, and use different parts of speech correctly including nouns, verbs, and adjectives.

States and schools have their own standardized testing to assess students' reading skills. These metrics might be included in your branch community's dashboard; however, we recommend these metrics be summarized by grade (combining the schools) to the branch community level. By including the entire branch community we are engaging the entire community rather than just the children of the individual school. Figure 10.2 presents our recommended starter dashboard.

While these metrics are important for establishing a community benchmark, they are mostly reactive as opposed to proactive. In fact, Common Core has become a lightning rod of dissent in my own state of Oklahoma, where a large percent of third graders are at risk of being held back due to the controversial Common Core testing approach and the resulting poor reading scores. The third graders in Oklahoma may see reading as an obstacle to overcome and a thing to be feared, not something to enjoy and a path to success. We want dashboard metrics that allow us to respond before it is too late, metrics that go to the heart of the issue, and metrics that show a cause-and-effect relationship. For example, if a child likes to read and has found an author or subject she likes, there is a good chance she will become functionally literate as an adult.

Stephen D. Krashen, professor emeritus at the University of Southern California and leading figure on literacy and reading for pleasure, states,

> While children read for pleasure, when they get "hooked on books," they acquire, involuntarily and without conscious effort, nearly all of the so-called "language skills" many people are so concerned about: they will become adequate readers, acquire a large vocabulary, develop the ability to understand and use complex grammatical constructions, develop a good writing style, and become good (but not necessarily perfect) spellers. Although free voluntary reading alone will not ensure attainment of the highest levels of literacy, it will at least ensure an acceptable level. Without it, I suspect the children simply do not have a chance.[18]

Krashen further states,

> Contrary to popular opinion, there is no evidence that teenagers are less engaged in literacy activities today than teenagers of the past. Teenagers today do just as much book reading as teenagers did 65 years ago, and it appears that they are more involved in reading and writing in general when we include computer use in the analysis. The true problem in literacy is not related to convincing reluctant teenagers to read: It is providing access to books for those living in poverty.[19]

If Krashen is correct, public libraries are the solution. Once again we recommend a proactive metric geared toward helping those students deemed at risk. At-risk students could range from those who do not like to read on one end to those who have dyslexia on the other end. The local school librarians, the local branch librarian, and community resources together would seek, engage, and transform these at-risk students.

A great example of this approach to seek, engage, and transform at-risk kids appeared in my local Tulsa newspaper. The article is from the *Tulsa World* about the Tulsa Shock, our woman's professional basketball team. Here are some excerpts from the article:

> Tulsa Shock basketball players Glory Johnson and Jennifer Lacy want Tulsa's youth to know that reading books can be just as exciting as playing sports. "We want younger kids to see that even the athletes are doing it," Johnson said. "It's not just something that your teachers and your parents are telling you to do. It's something that's going to help you grow and develop as you get older." Johnson and Lacy hosted the Shock's yearly storytime Tuesday afternoon at the Rudisill Regional Library as part of the Tulsa City-County Library's children and teen summer reading programs. . . .

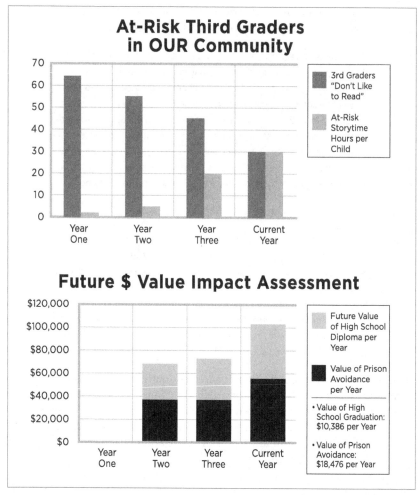

FIGURE 10.3
Love of Reading dashboard

. . . Tulsa City-County Library Children's Services Coordinator Lenore St. John said the Tulsa Shock's partnership helps give children the push they need to start and keep reading. Children who complete the library's summer reading program will receive free tickets to see the Shock play the Los Angeles Sparks at the BOK Center on Aug. 2, among other prizes, she said. [20]

I found it interesting that the article pointed out that both Johnson and Lacy did not like reading as a child, their only experience was from their perspective the unwelcome chore of developing book reports. As adults, they now fully recognize the importance of making reading fun for children. Figure 10.3 shows the love of reading program sample dashboard and its subsequent community future impact valuation.

POTTER'S PERSPECTIVE, POINTS, AND PONDERINGS— STUDENT'S LITERACY

Those of us who have been engaged in literacy efforts know that third grade is a critical moment in determining the long-term future for a student. While some question the point, many are certain that low childhood-literacy scores are an early indicator of long-term failure for that student. In fact, as John indicates, many suggest that failure to reach necessary literacy levels in elementary school can be in indicator of future prison populations.[21] Perhaps a better way to make this point is that it is around this time when readers stop learning to read and start reading to learn. If that foundation is not in place, a student can expect struggles in the remaining school years.

Mid-Continent Public Library believes that literacy is a very broad area. It is much more than reading. Literacy includes writing, expressing an idea, and understanding others' ideas. This more holistic approach to literacy is the basis for our Story Center at Woodneath. We will explore this much more in chapter 21.

A problem that schools have right now is that they are required to operate within a very rigid framework. There are standardized tests, state standards, No Child Left Behind, and now Common Core. These standards tend to encourage schools to focus on what is needed to meet the standard. But what if people are not able to learn through this process? Public libraries may be ideally positioned to fill the learning gap. I have two examples.

First, many parents find that the school environment does not fit well with their child's learning and the best alternative is to homeschool their child. When this happens, the local public library frequently becomes the academic support services for the family's efforts. There are countless reasons why a family decides to take on this great responsibility. Regardless of the reason, it seems that most all of them use the library. I believe it is very important to develop a positive working relationship with homeschool families. The relationship must provide a win-win situation. The library cannot become the de facto "school" for the homeschoolers because the library staff are neither trained nor equipped to take on that kind of responsibility. But the library should work closely with homeschoolers to help provide opportunities for their students.

Second, I believe that public libraries are ideally suited to help support educational opportunities that schools sometimes cannot support. MCPL was

recently approached about helping to support National History Day (www
.nhd.org) contests in our area. This really is the history equivalent of the science fair or spelling bee that involves students researching and presenting
information on historical topics. But, unlike the science fair or spelling bee,
this program seems to only sustain in a school as long as a teacher is willing to
participate. If classroom requirements change or if that teacher is transferred,
students from that school may no longer be able to participate. We are still
working on this partnership, but the idea is that we could introduce children
to the library's resources, including our historical newspaper and archive collections, and create learning opportunities that are attractive to some students. Depending on the students and their individual likes, this could be the
program that facilitates the transition to "reading to learn." At the very least,
it helps guard against that famous warning from Harry S. Truman, "The only
thing new in the world is the history you don't know."

Key to all of this, however, is very close relationships and cooperation
between schools and libraries. This is a very fine point but one that must be
made. Public libraries and school library media centers are different. I don't
think one can or should be substituted for the other. In general, I think it is a
mistake to try to combine a school library and a public library.

However, realizing that these institutions are both working to help people become more literate, we need to work together. I have seen many models
for this. The Clay County (MO) Economic Development Council created the
Northland Education and Business Alliance (www.clayedc.com/AboutEDC/
EdcCommittees/schools.html) several years ago to facilitate communication
between schools and businesses. I know you can find organizations like this
in your community. It may be your chamber of commerce, economic development corporation, or another organization. If schools and businesses are
already talking, get yourself invited to those meetings. If they aren't already
talking, invite them to coffee one morning and start the conversation.

At the very least, as the public librarian, you need to reach out to the
schools to share with them how we can all work together. There is a lot that we
can share with schools. If we work together, we can accomplish great things.

ADULT FUNCTIONAL LITERACY

For the definition of *adult functional literacy* we look to the National Center for
Education Statistics (NCES):

> **Prose Literacy.** The knowledge and skills to search, comprehend, and
> use continuous texts (e.g., editorials, news stories, brochures, and
> instructional materials)

Document Literacy. The knowledge and skills to search, comprehend, and use noncontinuous texts in various formats (e.g., job applications, payroll forms, transportation schedules, maps, tables, and drug or food labels)

Quantitative Literacy. The knowledge and skills to identify and perform computations using numbers embedded in printed materials (e.g., balancing a checkbook, calculating a tip)[22]

In 2003 NCES sponsored the nation's most comprehensive measure of adult literacy, the National Assessment of Adult Literacy (NAAL). With an estimated population of 216 million (for people 16 years and older), 14 percent, or 30 million individuals, performed below basic prose literacy in 2003. Fifty-five percent of adults with below-basic prose literacy did not graduate from high school, compared to 15 percent of adults in the general population.[23]

While the study is more than a decade old, I believe when considering the past few years' economic climate we can assume that the data now is similar if not worse.

The *Plain Language at Work Newsletter* provided a solid assessment of this issue:

Those with Below Basic reading skills cannot:

- Understand the instructions on a medicine container

- Read stories to their children

- Read a newspaper article or a map

- Read correspondence from their bank or any government agency

- Fill out an application for work

- Read the safety instructions for operating machinery

- Compete effectively for today's jobs

Forty-three percent of adults with low literacy skills live in poverty, 17% receive food stamps, and 70% have no job or part-time job. Over 60% of front-line workers in the goods-producing sector have difficulty applying information from a text to a required task.

More than 20% of adults read at or below the fifth-grade level, far below the level needed to earn a living wage. Adults at Level 1 earned a median income of $240 per week, compared to $681 for those at Level 5. Seventy percent of prisoners are in the two lowest levels.

The studies show that low literacy is not primarily the problem of immigrants, the elderly, high school dropouts, or people whose first language is not English. Low literacy is a problem that knows no age, education, economic boundaries, or national origins. Most people with

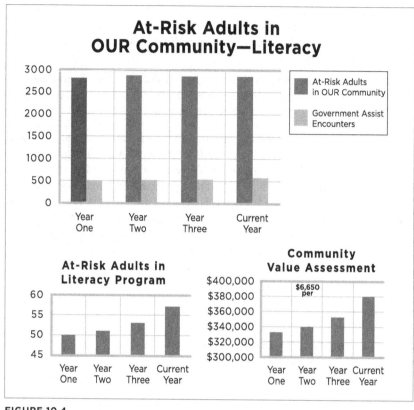

FIGURE 10.4
Adult literacy

low literacy skills were born in this country or have English as their first language.

It does no good to complain, "the schools are not doing their job." Over 80% of the year 2000 workforce are already out of school. It is a problem that industry, schools, health providers, churches, libraries, and public agencies must address aggressively."[24]

Furthermore, NCES used the NAAL data to project literacy levels to individual state and counties. For example, NCES estimates 14 percent of Tulsa County adults lack basic prose literacy skills, Los Angeles County—33 percent, Humboldt County—9 percent, El Paso County (CO)—9 percent, Queens County (NY)—46 percent, Jackson County (Kansas City, MO)—8 percent, Dallas County—21 percent. You can visit http://nces.ed.gov/naal/estimates/StateEstimates.aspx to view your own county's results.[25]

If we can assume this dated material provides an accurate assessment on today's population and that the projections have some validity, we can conclude that the adult literacy segment of our pyramid is missing a few bricks in its foundation. Depending on your community, the NCES estimates anywhere from 8 to 46 percent of the foundation we wish to build our pyramid upon is missing.

Adults at risk are more difficult to seek and engage than students or even preschoolers. To find these adults who have difficulty climbing past the first step of the pyramid I once again look toward the local branch staff. Library staff members tell me local, state, and federal departments are relying more and more on libraries to assist community members with filling out government forms. While this could be seen as a burden, we see it as an opportunity. Through face-to-face interactions, staff can identify, seek, and engage at-risk adults and offer community-sponsored education programs or library-sponsored programs and software. In addition, businesses can help their at-risk employees by connecting them to the library. It will take other proactive and creative ideas like partnering with charitable groups or combining resources with the local community colleges to impact adult literacy.

In figure 10.4, OUR fictitious dashboard for adult functional literacy, we use the stated 14 percent adult illiteracy rate for our community as well as the estimated cost to our nation of $225 billion per year from nonproductivity in the workforce, crime, and loss of tax revenue due to unemployment.[26]

POTTER'S PERSPECTIVE, POINTS, AND PONDERINGS—ADULT FUNCTIONAL LITERACY

I was recently asked to judge rounds at a high school debate tournament. I happened to be assigned to a room that was used for English. I noticed that the teacher had a chart on the wall with multi-digit numbers down the left side (e.g., 753924) and a listing of grades across the top (e.g., fifth, sixth, seventh). I determined this was actually a scorecard of the grade-level reading in this high school classroom. What was surprising was that there were only two people marked as eleventh or twelfth grade. Most people were solidly in what we might consider upper elementary grades. Sadly, a lot were in the lower elementary level. I can't shake this image. I realize that many of the children in the classroom are going to be the adults of the future with long-term literacy issues.

One thing I discovered many years ago is that many people are working to address the issue of adult literacy. In fact, I suggest the largest issue is that everyone is trying to reinvent the wheel. Resources are too precious to do this. If it hasn't already been done, the library in your community should convene a meeting of all the groups touching issues of adult literacy. Once this is done, figure out who needs to lead, who needs to support, and what is currently being duplicated. The library is the focal point for literacy; it should therefore be the focal point for adult literacy as well.

When we started working on our market segments, we made a very interesting discovery. As introduced in figure 6.3, we found a group of customers we named Early & Often. This group consists of parents with small children. They visit the library early in their child's life and sometimes more than once a week. These parents clearly "got the memo." They understand that their children are more likely to succeed in school with programs like Head Start, Parents as Teachers, and participation in library storytimes. We also discovered a group of library users we named Point & Click. These library users are very similar to the Early & Often parents. They have young children, and they visit the library frequently. However, they borrow very little. They see the library as a community computer center. Library employees know about Point & Click customers. Frequently you see them with their children sitting at their feet, unplugging other customers' computers. Or sometimes you find that you are retrieving their children and bringing them back to the parent, going through your standard, "the library isn't a safe place for little kids to be unsupervised" speech. These parents "didn't get the memo." I would venture to say that there is a third group of nonlibrary users out there with children who are not exposed to the library at all.

Why does this matter? For us, we discovered that we had a very strong base to build on. We also discovered that we had a lot of people with library awareness who didn't understand what the library could do for their children. For that group, we created programming that could, for example, teach enhanced computing skills while simultaneously running an early childhood literacy based program. This addressed our behavior problems and gave us a way to meet the needs of the Point & Click parent while constantly reinforcing the idea that early literacy is important. Part of our strategy is to move people from marginal market segments to engaged segments. In this case, the idea is to move many Point & Clicks to Early & Often. MCPL is cooperating with Literacy KC on a new program that will implement this concept. If we are fortunate, we will enhance many adults' functional literacy. Meanwhile, we will provide early childhood literacy training for their children disguised as "free child care." If we are successful, we will be able to break the cycle of illiteracy for participating families.

NOTES

1. "Read," Multnomah County Library, https://multcolib.org/parents/early-literacy/six-early-literacy-skills.

2. "The State of Preschool 2012: State Preschool Yearbook Press Conference," NIEER, April 2013, http://nieer.org/publications/presentations/state-preschool-2012-state-preschool-yearbook-press-conference.

3. Steven Herb and Sara Willoughby-Herb, "Preschool Education through Public Libraries," School Library Media Research 4 (2001), www.ala.org/aasl/aaslpubsandjournals/slmrb/slmrcontents/volume42001/herb.

4. Beth Kantor, "Why Preschool Matters," *Parents Magazine*, February 2007, www.parents.com/toddlers-preschoolers/starting-preschool/curriculum/why-preschool-matters.

5. W. Steven Barnett and Donald J. Yarosz, "Who Goes to Preschool and Why Does it Matter?" NIEER, Issue 15, revised November 2007, http://nieer.org/resources/policybriefs/15.pdf.

6. "Harris Interactive: Executive Summary of Survey Commissioned by RIF and Macy's," Reading Is Fundamental, 2013, www.scribd.com/doc/148798776/Harris-Interactive-Executive-Summary-of-Survey-Commissioned-by-RIF-and-Macy-s.

7. "Who's Minding the Kids? Child Care Arrangements," NACCRRA, Spring 2010, http://www.naccrra.org/sites/default/files/default_site_pages/2012/whos_minding_the_kids_feb_2012_0.pdf.

8. "High School Dropout Statistics," Statistics Brain, January 1, 2014, www.statisticbrain.com/high-school-dropout-statistics.

9. Ibid.

10. "The Price of Prisons: What Incarceration Costs Taxpayers—Oklahoma Fact Sheet" VERA Institute of Justice, January 2012, www.vera.org/files/price-of-prisons-oklahoma-fact-sheet.pdf.

11. Jason M. Breslow, "By the Numbers: Dropping Out of High School," WGBH, *Frontline*, September 21, 2012, www.pbs.org/wgbh/pages/frontline/education/dropout-nation/by-the-numbers-dropping-out-of-high-school.

12. "The State of Preschool 2012," NIEER.

13. "CAP Tulsa Featured on *CBS Evening News*," CAP Tulsa, May 2013, http://captulsa.org/cap-tulsa-featured-on-cbs-evening-news.

14. "Head Start Annual Report 2012–2013," CAP Tulsa, http://captulsa.org/wp/wp-content/uploads/2012/09/CAP-Annual-Report-2012.pdf.

15. "Early Reading Proficiency in the United States," Annie E. Casey Foundation, January 2010, www.aecf.org/m/resourcedoc/aecf-EarlyReadingProficiency-2014.pdf.

16. "Statistics about Education in America," StudentsFirst, www.studentsfirst.org/pages/the-stats.

17. "Reading to Learn: Upper Elementary Reading Skills," Scholastic, www.scholastic.com/parents/resources/article/milestones-expectations/reading-to-learn-upper-elementary-reading-skills.

18. Stephen Krashen, quoted in Christina Clark and Kate Rumbold, "Reading for Pleasure: A Research Overview," National Literacy Trust, November 2006, http://www.literacytrust.org.uk/assets/0000/0562/Reading_pleasure _2006.pdf.

19. Stephen Krashen, "Reading for Pleasure," *Language Magazine*, http://languagemagazine.com/?page_id=3031.

20. Samantha Vincent, "Tulsa Shock players score one for reading," *Tulsa World*, July 24, 2013, www.tulsaworld.com/news/local/tulsa-shock-players-score -one-for-reading/article_87edf195-fac6-5f0e-8452-ef32fd9a30f8.html.

21. Steve Cohen, "A $5 Children's Book vs. A $47,000 Jail Cell—Choose One," Forbes.com, December 20, 2013, www.forbes.com/sites/stevecohen/ 2010/12/25/a-5-childrens-book-vs-a-47000-jail-cell-choose-one.

22. "Three Types of Literacy," National Center for Education Statistics, http://nces.ed.gov/naal/literacytypes.asp.

23. "About Literacy," Vita Education Services, www.vitaeducation.org/our -programs/basic-education-programs/about-literacy.

24. William H. DuBay, "Know Your Reader," *Plain Language at Work Newsletter*, http://www.impact-information.com/impactinfo/literacy.htm. Reprinted with permission.

25. "National Assessment of Adult Literacy, State and County Estimates of Low Literacy," Institute of Education Services, National Center for Education Statistics, http://nces.ed.gov/naal/estimates/StateEstimates.aspx.

26. "The Cost of Low Literacy," Literacy Partners, www.literacypartners.org/ literacy-in-america/impact-of-illiteracy.

11
Digital Literacy and Access

I N THIS CHAPTER WE PROPOSE THAT DIGITAL LITERACY IS AS critical to your community's ability to advance up the pyramid as literacy itself. We present how digital literacy can be defined in the same terms as literacy and how it can be measured and tracked through simple dashboard metrics.

If you look at the steps of our community pyramid, you notice that each has Digital Literacy and Access as a component. Social networks, job networks, workplace computers, creative writing, digital art, research, knowledge development, and philanthropy all require knowledge of the digital landscape and its tools.

Using the NCES definition of literacy that we used earlier, we can create a similar definition of digital literacy including the categories of Basic, Functional, and Quantitative.

Basic Digital Literacy
- ability to turn on the computer and navigate its keyboard
- ability to access the library's website with username/card number and password

- ability to safely access web information, practice net etiquette, and manage/avoid cyberbullying
- ability to safely communicate online with friends and family
- ability to use educational programs for math, science, and reading

Functional Digital Literacy

- ability to use basic functions of programs such as Word, Excel, and PowerPoint
- ability to perform surface web research
- ability to complete civic and job application forms
- ability to safely access and download popular and specialized print and video media
- ability to develop a safe online presence, such as blogs, resumes, and social networks
- ability to safely access businesses online to manage bank accounts and purchase and sell goods

Quantitative Digital Literacy

- ability to use advanced functions of programs such as Word, Excel, and PowerPoint
- ability to access and perform deep web research employing online critical-thinking skills

In chapter 10 our dashboard metrics focused on seeking out, engaging, and transforming community members who struggle with basic and functional literacy. We must do the same for digital literacy.

In Kenya, around one smoky kerosene lamp, brothers and sisters huddled to read and study. That was until Evans Wadongo came up with a better idea.

> I couldn't compete effectively with other kids who had access to lighting," he said. "In every home in the village it was the same. Many children drop out of school for these reasons . . . so they remain poor for the rest of their life. All along I was asking myself if there is anything that can be done to improve this situation.[1]

Wadongo did find a way. As a student at Kenya University he invented an inexpensive LED solar lamp that has transformed rural villages across his country.

It is pretty simple; children who have light to study and read by at night have a significant advantage over children who do not. Children who have access to a computer and broadband internet access at night have a distinct advantage over children who do not.

"While computers help adults looking for jobs and assist students to do better in school, about 30 percent of Americans don't have home computers," said Bob Grove, spokesman for Comcast Corp in 2012.[2] In 2013, about 26 percent of all households reported no internet use, with 73.4 percent reporting a high-speed connection. Specifically, about 38 percent of this group have income less than $25,000 per year, and 57 percent have no high school diploma. Approximately 40 percent of all African-American and 34 percent of Hispanic households do not have wired internet access at home, compared with 24 percent of whites.[3]

Library patrons who are at risk for digital illiteracy are well known to the library staff. Library staffs who assist the public computer centers constantly engage with those who need help with simple and basic skills such as how to log in, create an e-mail account, and access the internet. These patrons are our target group. If the library coordinates with charitable groups, local businesses, and government service groups, additional at-risk adults can be identified and offered assistance.

While discussing this topic with Steve, he shared a story with me. A couple of years ago the Piper School District (KS) gave all their students laptops, but something unexpected happened. Each day before school started, scores of kids sat outside their school building doing their homework because they couldn't access the internet at home. A similar situation occurred in the nearby North Kansas City School District. In response, the North Kansas City School District outfitted many school buses with Wi-Fi so kids could do homework to and from school.

Access to public computers and the internet has been a high priority for public libraries. Under budget constraints, let us hope that public libraries in at-risk communities do not close their doors at 5 p.m. At-risk students need an even playing field, and the only option they have may be the public library.

The difference between functional literacy and functional digital literacy is that we encourage children to read for fun. To encourage a child to have fun on the computer translates into video games and social networking, so our read-for-fun concept for literacy does not quite translate to digital literacy. To have students gain basic, fundamental, and quantitative skills on the computer requires a disciplined curriculum, defined expectations, and perhaps some fun thrown in as well.

Just as we focused on at-risk children, students, and adults for functional literacy, we also focus on this same population for digital literacy. We must once again embrace Pikes Peak's mantra to seek, engage, and transform.

School librarians and public librarians can take the same approach in identifying these at-risk community members by coordinating their efforts with government services and local charities as well as their day-to-day experience in the school or community library. Just like with literacy, there are many computer-based programs available to assist in this effort. Microsoft, for example, provides a free online digital literacy course and assessment tool that aligns itself very well with the definition of our basic, fundamental, and quantitative levels of digital literacy. The courses offered include these topics:

- computer basics
- the internet and the World Wide Web
- productivity programs
- computer security and privacy
- digital lifestyles

The site also includes instructor guidelines:

> The Digital Literacy Curriculum can be adapted for classroom use or for self-paced study. This page provides instructors with additional

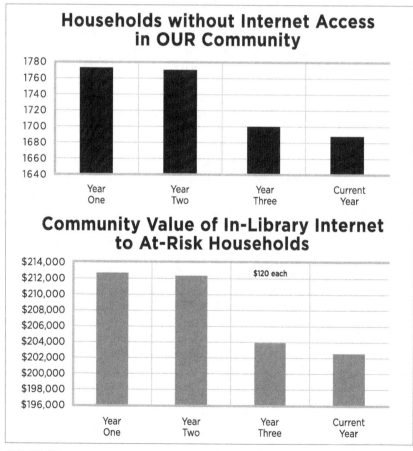

FIGURE 11.1

Digital access

resources to facilitate classroom use, including classroom setup information, teaching tips for each course, additional practice ideas, a test item file, and answers to frequently asked questions.[4]

Microsoft's digital literacy course and assessment tool drive our dashboard metrics. Figures 11.1 and 11.2 provide some examples for digital literacy dashboards to track your progress and understand key cause-and-effect community actions. We estimate the value of providing internet access to a low-income household to be $10 per month, or $120 per year.[5]

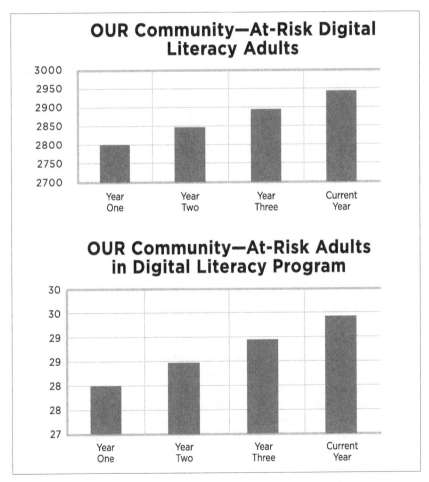

FIGURE 11.2
Digital literacy

POTTER'S PERSPECTIVE, POINTS, AND PONDERINGS

In this chapter we propose that digital literacy is as critical to your community's success as literacy itself and libraries must play a large role in this progression. I would like to share a few additional stories to drive home the point.

In the early 1990s I taught an Introduction to Information Technology course at the University of Missouri's library school. As we put the course together, we considered migrating it to an online environment. What would be more cutting-edge than to teach new technology in a new technology environment? But there was something very wrong about this concept. It was not technology that was critical to the course. Rather, the introduction and orientation were the critical variables. If you are going to teach someone about technology, that person must have a foundation to build upon. We as librarians must remind ourselves that the technology we provide to our patrons is not of value if we do not introduce them to this technology first.

For example, in Missouri, you can renew your license plate through an online service. This option not only allows you to avoid the DMV, it actually prints renewal stickers that are customized for your plates, decreasing the chance that your renewal sticker will be stolen. Why doesn't *everyone* do this? In many cases they do not understand how to make the technology work. That's where the library can step in. We show people not only how technology can make their life easier, but in some very important cases, we even teach people the necessary skills they need to interact in today's world.

On May 22, 2011, during dinnertime the 50,000 residents of Joplin, Missouri, took shelter as an EF-5 tornado ripped through their town. For those who have seen the pictures, or saw it in person, you know the devastation this tornado reaped. I contacted my friend Jacque Gage, the director at Joplin Public Library, to see how MCPL could help her. I assumed her first request would be for water, blankets, and staff resource help. She wanted power strips. Why? The library had become a primary place for people to charge cell phones so they could connect to the outside world. She also needed more networked computers and bandwidth so the citizens of Joplin could file their online FEMA and SEMA forms. Yes, they needed water and clothes and food. But they also needed a significant bump in technology and they needed it *now*! Knowing technology, being technology literate, and having access to this technology may be much more a necessity than a luxury in cases like these. I cannot believe this situation will become less the case in the future.

Around Christmastime, while at Barnes & Noble, I discovered near the Nooks displays a stack of MCPL photocopied business cards. When I asked one of the B&N staff about the little stack of photocopied cards, she said, "This is who you need to call if you need help with your Nook after you buy it." That was interesting. So, I asked the MCPL branch manager whose card had been copied if he had set something up with B&N. He had not. But he had been wondering why so many people kept coming to him to help set up their e-book readers!

Whether we like it or not, people see technology support and education as a part of our role. Why fight it? Why not help build a foundation of strong technology literacy skills for your community? It is clear to me that delivery of information is migrating to a technology-based platform. If we are in the business of providing information to people, there will always be those that need help migrating from one medium to another or from one delivery system to another. As we help people migrate to new technology, we show them the relevance of the modern library. We create new relationships with people who can't live without us. How can that be a bad thing?

To this end, I think libraries can help people connect by showing them that there are new (and in some ways better) ways to do everyday tasks. There is no reason to wait until a tornado wipes out your town to worry about digital literacy.

NOTES

1. "Saving lives with solar-powered lights," *CNN.com*, February 12, 2010, www.cnn.com/2010/LIVING/02/11/cnnheroes.wadongo/index.html.
2. Denise Allabaugh, "Computer Skills Become Essential Tool for Job Seekers," April 1, 2012, http://thetimes-tribune.com/news/business/computer-skills-become-essential-tool-for-job-seekers.1293372.
3. Thom File and Camile Ryan, "Computer and Internet Use in the United States: 2013," November 2014, www.census.gov/content/dam/Census/library/publications/2014/acs/acs-28.pdf.
4. "Digital Literacy Instructor," Microsoft, www.microsoft.com/about/corporate citizenship/citizenship/giving/programs/up/digitalliteracy/eng/resources .mspx.
5. Cecelia Kang, "Comcast Is Trying to Improve Its Image with a Program for Low-Income Consumers," *Washington Post*, May 9, 2014, www.washingtonpost .com/business/technology/comcast-is-trying-to-improve-its-image-with-a -program-for-low-income-consumers/2014/05/09/cab489cc-d231–11e3 –937f-d3026234b51c_story.html.

12
Social Community Engagement

IN THIS CHAPTER WE EXAMINE HOW OUR COMMUNITIES ARE transforming from physical communities to virtual communities and how this trend creates a great risk to the health and well-being of your branch community and its members. We propose that libraries can fill this gap by being the focal point for your community for not only physical social interaction but virtual interaction as well. We discuss how there are those in your community who cannot progress up the pyramid past the Social Community Engagement step due to a lack of access to your social community and libraries can play a proactive role in filling these gaps. We present simple and effective dashboard metrics to track your progress.

I have a high school acquaintance who lives with her husband in an isolated cabin in the woods of Moose Jaw, Saskatchewan. She is the most prolific Facebook-posting friend I have. It appears from her posts that to physically talk face-to-face with another person besides her husband takes some planning. Facebook has become her connection to her virtual community. Her posts are about stunning landscapes, incredible snowfalls, vigorous and at times dangerous wildlife, and her thoughts on philosophy. She included this in a recent post: "Who says Facebook friends are not your real friends? They enjoy seeing you on the internet every day. Miss you when you're not on.

Showing compassion when you lose someone you love. Send you greetings on your birthday. View the pictures you upload. Like your status. Make you laugh when you are sad."

I understand my friend's need for community, and often the online community is her only immediate option. However if you examine your children during dinner, you might think we all live in Moose Jaw, relying on the online community for our social connection.

John Cacioppo, author of *The Need for Social Connection*, in an interview for *U.S. News & World Report's* Health website states:

> People have thought of (online social networks) as being all good or all bad, but it's more subtle than that. If you use artificial means of connecting as a substitute for physical means of connection, you actually get lonelier. However, if you are disabled and isolated by virtue of the disability and the Internet is permitting you to make connections, then it decreases feelings of isolation.[1]

We have defined the branch community library as our nexus point. While the online community is a virtual community with no physical boundaries, the community library is defined by geographical boundaries. One might argue that the need for geographically based communities has become an archaic idea. People with like interests can now choose whom they interact with no matter where they live. However, according to Cacioppo, people need more than this—they need to be physically near other people for their overall health and well-being.

Cacioppo further states in his interview:

> Early in human history, our species' survival required the protection of families and tribes. Isolation meant death. The painful feeling known as loneliness is a prompt to reconnect to others.
>
> Loneliness shows up in measurements of stress hormones, immune function, and cardiovascular function. Lonely adults consume more alcohol and get less exercise than those who are not lonely. Their diet is higher in fat, their sleep is less efficient, and they report more daytime fatigue. Loneliness also disrupts the regulation of cellular processes deep within the body, predisposing us to premature aging.[2]

Our community pyramid is at risk of people simply opting out. They could very easily live out their lives behind closed doors engaged in their online social world and never participate in a community gathering, a fireworks display, a book club, a kid's soccer game, the zoo, a neighborhood park, Sunday church, a night with friends, a local play, an art show, a drive-in movie, a neighborhood picnic, a job fair, a political debate, or a visit to their local library.

Our community pyramid would no longer be a pyramid but would be millions of separate silos, and the local physical community, a flat empty shell of itself, as in figure 12.1.

One night after one of my engagements working for the Kansas City Public Library, I noticed a program had been scheduled featuring a Mark Twain impersonator. Crosby Kemper III, the library director of KC Public, conducts a series of interviews with historical figures played by local actors and veteran Chautauqua performers. (Very cool.) I did not have the time to attend (as I was totally consumed redesigning the layout of their collection management group), but as I was walking out of their beautiful central library I observed the variety of people in the audience gathered for the event. Central and local libraries are the most accessible and perhaps one of the few diverse gathering places left in our community. Would the audience have the same experience if this Mark Twain event were simply a webcast? While providing a webcast of the event after the fact may be beneficial, a community's health and well-being depends on these face-to-face, diverse social gatherings. Imagine a community that was totally online and never met face-to-face. A good script for a science fiction film but a bad script for reality. (You can watch

FIGURE 12.1
Online community silos

Crosby's wonderful interview of "Mark Twain" at https://www.youtube.com/watch?v=baajoGjbxqQ.)

Online communities are not going away. Simply look at the number of magazine genres, multiply that by 100,000, and you may just scratch the number of online communities available to the varied interests of your community members. People are organizing themselves along lines of interest and not by the place they live. The purpose-based library will recognize that online communities are here to stay and leverage this tool to build and strengthen their community.

At this point we have discussed five parts of the pyramid: Food and Shelter Safety Net, Safety and Security, Health and Nutrition, Functional Literacy and Access, Digital Literacy and Access. We will soon discuss Functional Skills Development, Community Contribution, Creative Expression, Advancement of Knowledge, and Community Expression and Philanthropy. For these rising steps to be successful, community members must become engaged and involved. The purpose-based library must go where their patrons are—online—to achieve the Social Community Engagement step. We propose that every library system add a portal to their website that links to their branch community library pyramid. The pyramid would allow their patrons to enter into the world of their local community. Tabs for each of the pyramid steps would invite them to explore the pyramid step's dashboard metrics and see upcoming events and educational programs. They would be able to link to books and media resources to learn more on that particular pyramid's topic, join in discussions on repairing and rebuilding those steps, join community groups, and volunteer their time and resources. The purpose-based library would engage their community online to encourage the members of the community to get involved face-to-face with other community members.

DIGITAL SOCIAL ENGAGEMENT

Is it too soon to declare that if you do not have an online presence you are invisible to your community? In some ways the answer is yes. For your community members, having an online presence might include an e-mail account, smartphone messenger, Facebook or Twitter account, personal web page, online resume, LinkedIn account, personal blog, links to personal writings and artwork, e-bay account, Match.com account, FriendFinder app, emergency app, retailer apps, community event app, library app, news app, restaurant finder app, and a volunteer match app, and we could go on and on. Online social networking has become the circuit board for our community communications.

While on a project with the Fort Worth Library I found myself in the middle of a government-assisted community. I was very impressed that this particular community library was located near the center of this at-risk community. While we installed our Holds Label Solution Software, I was able to observe that 100 percent of the 15 available public computers were being used for Facebook, e-mail, and video streaming. For a community lacking the bare essentials of Maslow's hierarchy of needs, connecting with others through social and entertainment media seemed a first priority for these community members. This might expose a failing in their community pyramid, but it speaks loudly to the need and importance for our branch community members to feel connected to their friends, family, and the community as a whole, especially those without a computer. This experience resonates with me as we progress past the basic needs segment of our pyramid and onto the middle segment of our pyramid, Physiological Needs and Social Engagement.

Pew research tells us that 89 percent of the 18–29 age group are engaged in social networking. As we reach the over-65 age group we drop to 49 percent.[3] To be fair, many of the older set may have no interest in joining social networks and see no benefit from these tools. However, with the majority of the community engaged in an online social environment, these seniors may find themselves more and more secluded from their family and friends and the community as a whole. My own parents who are 86 years old are missing out on much news about their family as well as those great pictures of their great-grandchildren. The online community provides a great opportunity for the elderly to reengage with their family and their community—if they just had some assistance getting there. (With my parents I have had success by showing them the research tools at the Genealogy Center at TCCL.)

Pew tells us that a part of our community population is not fully engaged online with their friends, family, and community members. Those who are not participating because of lack of skills, resources, or simple lack of access show a weakness in our pyramid. Libraries once again shine for providing a safe and secure environment for community members to meet, communicate, and participate in both online communities as well as on-site community events. The purpose-based library plays a key role in assuring all community members have the opportunity to engage with their community. Figure 12.2 shows a sample community engagement dashboard.

Throughout this book we have emphasized the importance of value-added metrics. In each of the pyramid steps thus far we have been able to assess a tangible dollar value to the efforts of the library and their community partners. The dashboard in figure 12.3 brings it all together by showing the number of community transformation programs initiated and in progress in OUR community. It also provides a summary of the community value assessment of all these programs.

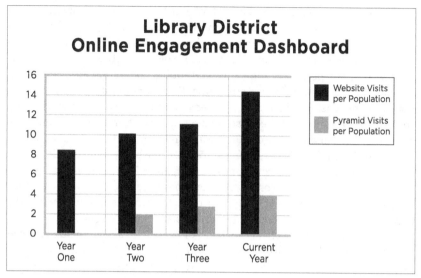

FIGURE 12.2
Community engagement

POTTER'S PERSPECTIVE, POINTS, AND PONDERINGS

In this chapter we discussed the migration from a physical world to a digital world and that some are being left behind. The migration to a digital world holds certain risks, and the library also plays a key role in addressing this risk. In the last half of the 20th century, our migration to a digital world created a new concept called *narrowcasting*. As opposed to broadcasting, narrowcasting is a concept where you focus narrowly and deeply on one idea or subject. This gave birth to television networks, like the History channel, Cooking Channel, and so on, that focus on one topic only. No news, no sports, no drama, no art. Eventually, this has morphed into a presentation of single, narrow worldview channels (CBN, Fox News, MSNBC, etc.).

Why does this matter? Libraries have always been about providing multiple points of view and sources of material and then letting the customer decide. However, in this environment of "narrowcasting," consumers are looking for experiences that reinforce their opinions and worldview. Libraries, unfairly, have been accused of taking one side or another simply because we present resources and information on all views and perspectives. This will never change but does present an image risk to us all.

Libraries must remain and constantly present themselves as apolitical. All political groups want their local community to be healthier. Yes, there are

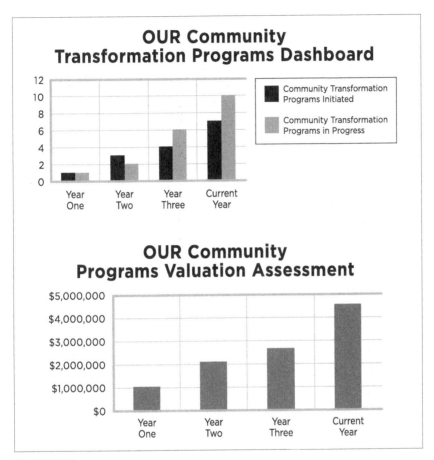

FIGURE 12.3
Community transformation

different opinions as to how this is to be done, but libraries can be seen as a positive and neutral force for change by simply serving as the community steward and archivist. As the community steward, libraries can provide the opportunity, resources, communications, and meeting rooms for the community to gather, both face-to-face and online, as they engage and transform.

NOTES

1. Nancy Shute, "Why Loneliness Is Bad for Your Health," *US News and World Report*, Health, November 12, 2008, http://health.usnews.com/health-news/

family-health/brain-and-behavior/articles/2008/11/12/why-loneliness-is-bad
-for-your-health.

2. Ibid.

3. "Social Networking Fact Sheet," Pew Research Internet Project, January 2014,
http://pewinternet.org/Commentary/2012/March/Pew-Internet-Social
-Networking-full-detail.aspx.

13
Functional Skills Development

I N THIS CHAPTER, WE PROGRESS UP OUR PYRAMID TO THE FUNC-
tional Skills Development step and address the need for community members to be functionally capable of contributing to their community. We examine how libraries are embracing new proactive concepts to assist their community members to improve and advance their functional skills as well as acquire tangible acknowledgment for their accomplishments. We present simple dashboard metrics to assess and track your progress and your contribution to helping these individuals advance their skills.

THE CURRENT STATE OF FUNCTIONAL SKILLS

We assume that everyone reading this book has composed his or her resume at one time or another. In fact, many of you have assisted others in developing their resume as a part of your job. Imagine how daunting a task this would be if you had no high school diploma, no relevant job experience, and no specific skills to mention. With the "new normal" unemployment rate, a resume such as this will not help this individual get a job, and more than likely this person would not even bother writing one in the first place. In the context of our community pyramid, this individual will find it difficult to contribute to our healthy and thriving community. In fact, we can surmise this individual is at risk of becoming a negative influence on our community and perhaps even becoming part of the welfare system, penal system, or homeless population.

Regarding incarceration rates, an August 2012 article from the Population Reference Bureau website states:

- The United States has had the highest incarceration rate in the world since 2002.

- The natural rate of incarceration for countries comparable to the United States is about 100 prisoners per 100,000 residents. In 2010 the US rate was 500 prisoners per 100,000 residents, about 1.6 million prisoners.

- Men make up 90 percent of the prison and local jail population, with an imprisonment rate 14 times higher than that of women.

- Incarceration rates are highest for men in their 20s and early 30s.

- The average state prisoner has a 10th grade education, and about 70 percent did not complete high school.[1]

Canada's Homelessness Resource Center states:

- In Canada, the more educated a people are, the less likely they are to live in poverty. In mid-sized cities, 21.4 percent of those with less than secondary school live in poverty as opposed to only 7 percent of those with a university degree.

- Individuals with relatively low levels of education are finding that jobs in the labor market increasingly go to more highly skilled workers.

- Among homeless people, many have not completed high school, and income support is often difficult to access. Those who receive social assistance often face landlords who will not accept them or require substantial deposits in advance.

- Many homeless people survive by panhandling, squeegeeing, and the sex trade because being homeless makes it very difficult to obtain and maintain formal employment and they often do not have the applicable skills or experience required to find a job that pays a living wage.[2]

The message is that catching those at-risk individuals while they are young becomes of paramount importance. For these adults the pyramid is nearly impossible to climb, and many fall into the community's food and shelter safety net.

LIBRARY-SPONSORED CONTINUING EDUCATION

Transforming those in our community who struggle to climb the pyramid into contributing members of society is a community's most difficult task and one would argue one of the most important. For these struggling adults (who are not drug addicted or mentally challenged) there is only one real option that can lead to positive results—that is continuing adult education. Considering the footprint of public libraries and the resources they provide, no one is better positioned to help these struggling adults than public libraries.

In previous chapters we have addressed literacy, digital literacy, and social connection. To obtain a job, these fundamental skills can help those seeking employment, but barely. Imagine a resume that says, I can read at a fundamental level, and I can check my e-mail and Facebook accounts, but I have no high school diploma and no effective job skills.

To assist these struggling community members, there must be a path outside the normal school system, a means to advance their skills and be recognized for this advancement. One example of this is the Los Angeles Public Library (LAPL), which recently partnered with the Career Online High School. A CBS News article explains the program:

> The Los Angeles Public Library is evolving from a place where people can check out books and surf the Web to one where residents can also earn an accredited high school diploma. . . . [LAPL offers over] 850 online courses for continuing education and . . . a program that helps immigrants complete the requirements for U.S. citizenship. The library hopes to grant high school diplomas to 150 adults in the first year at a cost to the library of $150,000.[3]

Director John Szabo is certainly committed to the program, for he states, "I believe with every cell in my body that public libraries absolutely change lives and change lives in very big ways." This program is special because it not only offers a real high school diploma, but also career skills courses. When you graduate from high school you will also have training and credentials as a certified nursing assistant or a medical records technician, for example.

Steve and I believe this is only the beginning of an exciting continuing education path that libraries can sponsor. Over the years I have formed and served as the facilitator for countless cross-functional teams to streamline business processes. My manufacturing client's team members might include a maintenance worker, an assembly line worker, a supervisor, a press operator, a paint booth operator, and a material handler. I have found that the skill sets required to participate in these teams were often lacking. More often than not, the members of my teams had never been exposed to or asked to develop team-building skills. No one had taught these workers how to brainstorm together, how to solve problems together, or even how best to communicate with one another. In some cases I found the same thing with my library clients. To close this gap I conduct team-building workshops. These workshops include how to brainstorm as a group, how to approach and solve a problem, how to manage a project, how to collect data, how to understand and present data, and how to tap into their creative self. These skills are highly valued by today's organizations and would go a long way to stand out on a resume and in a job interview.

I envision a library-sponsored course for team communication and problem-solving skills to include:

Communication

- How to be respectful to your other team members
- How to listen
- How to ask open-ended questions
- How to add value, not argument

Team participation skills

- How to assist in organizing a project including agendas, project milestones, tasks-accomplished tracking, and open-issues management
- How to brainstorm
- How to solve problems as a group
- How to perform gap analysis

Creativity training

- How to be creative
- Tools of creativity

Dashboard metrics

- Pareto analysis (80/20 rule) (see chapter 17)
- Data collection, surveys, simple audits
- Pie charts
- Line and bar charts
- Simple Excel charts

There are many other areas of continuing education that can be sponsored by libraries, many of which you are already engaged in. Each community library should tailor their online programs to the needs of their community's unique needs and opportunities. Taking LAPL's example, these online courses could be provided by creating partnerships with organizations such as the Career

Online High School. The programs would be provided and administered by the community branch library targeting those individuals looking for jobs or wishing to increase their workplace skills. The program would also be made available to all school and academic libraries.

THE FUTURE

We have discussed those adults in our society who lack the basic skills to contribute to our community's health and well-being. Unfortunately, this group may grow dramatically in the future.

According to the International Federation of Robotics,

> In 2012, about 28,100 industrial robots were shipped to the Americas, 7% more than in 2011, reaching a new peak level. Since 2010, the modernization of the North American factories and the increase of production capacities in North America and in Brazil, especially by the automotive industry, accelerated the pace of robot installations substantially.[4]

Robotics and technology are already changing the landscape of today's job market. A recent *DailyMail.com* article asks, "Is 2014 the year YOUR job will be taken by a robot? 'Jobocalpyse' [sic] set to strike as droids are trained to flip burgers, pour drinks—and even look after our children." The article predicts:

- 70 percent of occupations could become automated over next 30 years.
- Servers, bartenders, cooks, drivers, teachers, babysitters, and nurses could be replaced by robots.

It further states, "In China there is already the Robot Restaurant, where 20 robots deliver food to the table, cook dumplings and noodles, usher diners and entertain them." And it says that a San Francisco robotics firm has a "burger-flipping robot . . . able to make 360 hamburgers per hour. It can make custom burgers for each customer, and the firm says it is 'more consistent and more sanitary' than human workers. 'Our alpha machine frees up all of the hamburger line cooks in a restaurant." The firm intends to open a San Francisco restaurant that uses this technology and hopes to sell it to existing burger chains.[5]

This is only the beginning. Innovation is pressing at an exponential pace, and in the next 20 years the job market will be totally different than today. Imagine if Walmart and the fast food industry cut their staff by 50 to 90 percent. The gap between those less educated and those highly educated (and consequently those who are poor and those who are rich) is already wide. This

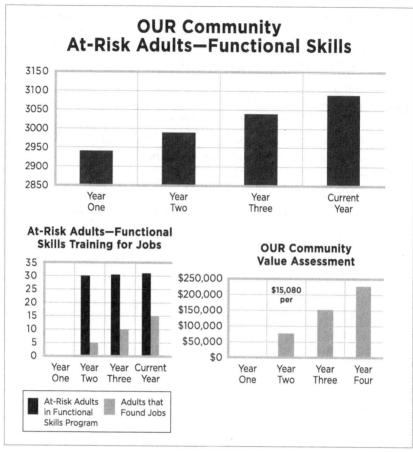

FIGURE 13.1

Adult functional literacy

gap will also grow at an exponential rate if actions are not taken soon to prepare these adults for the coming new job market, specifically through responsive adult education.

As the article predicts, 70 percent of current jobs may be affected in the next 30 years. We should not hide the fact that on the library's current path of touchless customer service, librarians are well on their path to be included in the 70-percent number. However, this path can be redirected if your library becomes a purpose-based library. One could argue the need for adult continuing education would make libraries one of the most valuable future assets a community can invest in.

For OUR imaginary community dashboard we valued the number of adults that found jobs as a result of the library's training and job placement activities at $15,080[6] per placement, the value of a minimum wage job. Figure 13.1 shows an adult functional literacy dashboard.

NOTES

1. Tyjen Tsai and Paola Scommegna, "U.S. Has World's Highest Incarceration Rate," Population Reference Bureau, August 2012, www.prb.org/Publications/Articles/2012/us-incarceration.aspx.

2. Asetha Power, "CHHEnglish: Income, Employment & Education," Homelessness Resource Center, 2008, http://homeless.samhsa.gov/channel/income-employment-and-education-178.aspx.

3. "LA Public Library to Offer High School Diplomas," CBS Los Angeles, January 9, 2014, http://losangeles.cbslocal.com/2014/01/09/la-public-library-to-offer-high-school-diplomas.

4. "Industrial Robot Statistics, World Robotics 2014: Industrial Robots," International Federation of Robotics, www.ifr.org/industrial-robots/statistics.

5. Mark Prigg, "Is 2014 the Year YOUR Job Will Be Taken by a Robot? 'Jobocalpyse' [sic] Set to Strike as Droids Are Trained to Flip Burgers, Pour Drinks—and Even Look After Our Children," *DailyMail.com*, last updated January 21, 2014, www.dailymail.co.uk/sciencetech/article-2542113/Will-robot-jobocalypse-make-YOU-obsolete-2014-year-droid-takes-job-say-experts.html.

6. David Sessions, "Five Things You Didn't Know about the Minimum Wage," *The Daily Beast*, February 15, 2013, www.thedailybeast.com/articles/2013/02/15/five-things-you-didn-t-know-about-the-minimum-wage.html.

14
Community Contribution

IN THIS CHAPTER WE EXAMINE THE LIBRARY'S COMMUNITY transformation efforts for the Community Contribution step of the pyramid. We propose that business incubators are still a viable idea. We also discuss how libraries' vast experience with internal internship programs well positions them to sponsor external internship programs for those seeking employment. Once again, we present simple dashboard metrics to guide your way.

Up to this point, we have formed our pyramid by building a safe and healthy community with skill sets in literacy, digital literacy, social engagement, and functional skills (continuing adult education). These skill sets provide our community members the opportunity to contribute to the health and well-being of their community. These contributions can take many forms, including:

- Starting a new business
- Contributing to the success of a business through employment
- Volunteering
- Paying taxes

The purpose-based library plays a key role in all of these processes, including business incubation, employment assistance, volunteer assistance, and local business partnerships.

BUSINESS INCUBATORS

In October 1986 I started J. Huber & Associates. It was a daunting task, as in a few short weeks I had to overcome a very large learning curve. I needed to incorporate, file state and federal forms, find an office, buy a printer, buy a fax machine, buy supplies, and hire and train employees. The best decision I made was to locate my office in a business center that included 30 other small businesses. We shared a receptionist, an administrative assistant, a phone system, and a common purpose of success and growth. On the floor I found a lawyer, a human resources outplacement firm, an investment broker, and many other helpful resources. It was a great environment in which to share, learn, and survive.

Libraries are, of course, a perfect business incubator. Arizona State University recognized this potential and plans to create a network of "coworking" business incubators inside public libraries. The downtown Civic Center Library in Scottsdale is their pilot. They plan to host dedicated coworking spaces as well as provide informal mentoring from the university's entrepreneurial resources.[1]

Incubators have been around the library world for many years. Some have failed; some have succeeded. Those that succeed often follow the examples of for-profit models, such as the coworking hives that are sprouting up across the country. From coast to coast, creative versions of for-profit business incubators are flourishing. *Inc.com*'s article "16 Cool Coworking Spaces" presents creative coworking spaces with rental fees ranging from $50 to $200 per month. "They're affordable, full of start-up geeks like you, and way cooler than any office you could afford," states author Christina DesMarais. From a boutique in a historic Boston neighborhood to outdoor spaces in Austin to concierge services in Minneapolis to woman-focused spa-themed spaces in San Diego to work-for-your-rent spaces in Chandler, Arizona, these incubator spaces are thriving.[2]

Libraries already have unique spaces equipped with everything a business incubator needs. It is only a matter of embracing the concept and putting your unique community twist on how it is presented. Partnering with local universities adds to the chances of success. Oklahoma State University has one of the top entrepreneurial programs in the country, which could make it a natural partner for the Tulsa and Oklahoma City public library's incubator efforts.

However, physical space is not the only business incubator concept available to public libraries. For example, Mid-Continent Public Library looked outside their four walls and created a virtual gateway of online resources for their incubator. Not only did it focus on the needs of a startup business, it also passed these entrepreneurs through automatically to MCPL's subscription

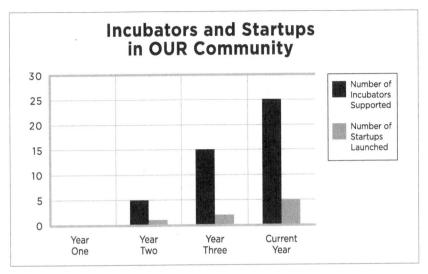

FIGURE 14.1
Business incubators

resources. MCPL's objective was to go where the customer is rather than force the customer to come to them. The idea of an online incubator resource is an idea worth considering for library websites. Figure 14.1 shows dashboard metrics for business incubators.

EMPLOYING THE SO-CALLED UNEMPLOYABLE

When I was 15, I worked for Arby's and developed a taste for their roast beef. During my out-of-town consulting projects I usually have time for a just a quick lunch, and I often choose Arby's. A year or so ago I noticed that at every Arby's I visited, no matter what city or state I was in, I would encounter a worker with a disability. During lunch one day in my hometown of Tulsa, I just happened to run across one of their corporate personnel, as Tulsa is home to Arby's largest franchise. I asked him if hiring disabled workers was a corporate initiative. He told me no, it was not their program but that an organization that sponsored disabled workers had approached them with good candidates, so they included them in their recruiting pool. He added that they are great employees.

Arby's hired disabled workers because a group sponsored them. The Advocacy Resource Center (ARC) of Macon, Georgia, provides us a great example of such an organization. ARC explains their purpose on their website's home page:

> In 1998, The ARC of Macon began providing supported employment services in response to the many requests of the people we support to have real jobs in the community. A variety of services are offered to persons with developmental disabilities including job coaching, job analysis, and job development. Presently The ARC of Macon has 19 individuals working in the community and we are constantly contacting Middle Georgia employers in our attempts to increase the number of people assisted by our Supported Employment Program. We have created a network of alliances with such companies as Arby's, Burger King, Cheddar's, Kroger, The Macon Color Wheel, Wendy's, and YKK. These businesses continue to lead the way in the process of integration of employable individuals with disabilities into the community. Progress has been made but we still have a long way to go in our mission of educating the public that people with disabilities should be treated with respect and dignity, and should have every opportunity granted to you or me.[3]

Libraries have a long history assisting the unemployed develop resumes, conduct job searches, and prepare for job interviews. Considering the "new normal" and future robotic-driven unemployment rate, this service is in large demand. In the past chapters we identified numerous opportunities to partner with local community businesses to rebuild and repair your pyramid. For example, local businesses can provide free workshops from their human resources group, they can funnel at-risk adults in need of literacy and digital literacy assistance to the library, and they can benefit from job skills training programs, meeting spaces, business incubator tools, and resources the library offers. This provides an opportunity to create an even tighter relationship with your community businesses. Specifically, libraries can leverage these relationships to help job seekers enter the workforce through sponsored internships.

Arby's and many others are proof that organizations do exist in your local community dedicated to the health and well-being of your local pyramid. The ARC lesson is that people who have a hard time finding a job could find a job if they only had a sponsor. The purpose-based library can be that sponsor. To say it another way, we know that social networking is the key to finding a job. The community library can become that social network for their unemployed community members through the partnerships they develop with local businesses. In this light, we propose a library-sponsored intern program to facilitate these partnerships.

INTERNSHIPS

Having my own business as well as four kids who have completed college and are now employed, I understand the value of internship programs. Businesses gain greatly by hiring interns for a temporary time period. These programs create a recruiting pipeline for a business and a means to train and evaluate potential employees. Interns gain valuable job skills, real-world experience, and an expanded social network. Students often find an internship through family, friends, or college professors and typically in a professional environment such as a large corporation, an architecture firm, politics, or the law.

I believe we can learn from both the ARC program and internship programs and create an exciting new jobs program with the public library at the center. Working with local community businesses, the public library would identify the type of skill sets these local businesses seek. Those looking for work would match their interests with a particular intern who has completed continuing education credits in pre-targeted functional skills such as those we presented in the prior chapter. To complete their training, interns would be matched with one of these businesses and complete a four-week on-site intern program. Paid internships would be preferred, but that would be evaluated on a case-by-case basis. As part of the program, the business would be under no obligation to hire the intern at the end of the four weeks.

Even if a business supported just one intern a year and did not hire that intern, it would still be a huge value to the community. The skills and social network gained from the four-week engagement would be a priceless advantage for a job seeker. For example, moms who are reentering the workforce after years of being out of the game would have an opportunity to ease back into the business world through these internships. People who have no social network to rely on would have the opportunity to build their own social network. Businesses like Arby's understand the importance of community engagement and providing opportunities for those most challenged in our society. There are many, many businesses that if approached would sign up for this program to help those unemployed get back in the game.

The library and their local business partners would assure the program meets the internship guidelines established by the US Department of Labor:

1. The internship, even though it includes actual operation of the facilities of the employer, is similar to training which would be given in an educational environment.

2. The internship experience is for the benefit of the intern.

3. The intern does not displace regular employees, but works under close supervision of existing staff.

4. The employer that provides the training derives no immediate advantage from the activities of the intern; and on occasion its operations may actually be impeded.

5. The intern is not necessarily entitled to a job at the conclusion of the internship.

6. The employer and the intern understand that the intern is not entitled to wages for the time spent in the internship.[4]

Those seeking employment gain skills, an expanded social network, self-worth, and an improved resume. Local small businesses gain by having a

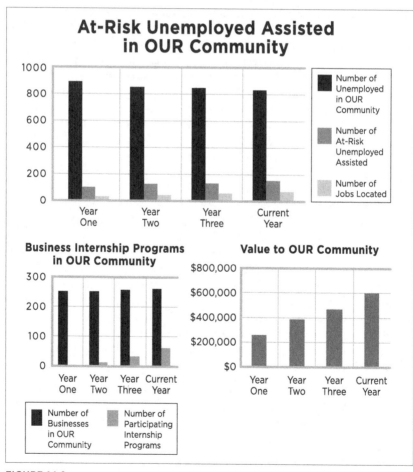

FIGURE 14.2
Unemployed

recruiting channel of trained and evaluated potential employees as well as a healthier pyramid.

Many of you who started your career as a library intern are familiar with the benefits, and Mid-Continent Public Library is no exception. But MCPL took the typical library internship and tweaked it by expanding their perspective on potential library interns. Steve provides some highlights of the program.

> MCPL has an active intern recruiting program, for example, we partnered with a local community college (that has more work-study money than they have opportunities) to fill our "computer lab assistants" positions. In addition we want to recruit interns with "child development" degrees and certificates for our early literacy storytimes.
>
> This program differs from a typical library internship or practicum in that MCPL does not look for MLS students to provide library experience. Instead, MCPL was looking for students with technology skills, maybe even studying computer science, to help bring additional skills and support to the computer labs. It exposes students to how technology is used in libraries. It provides skills to the library from young and bright minds. It provides better service to the public. All of these are positive outcomes.
>
> Through all these intern partnerships, everyone wins, including the library.

For OUR internship dashboard, shown in figure 14.2, we based our value assessment at $8,571 per intern per year, the cost of an unemployed worker for one year.[5]

VOLUNTEERS

Coming from the manufacturing world, the concept of volunteers in the workforce was a bit alien to me. Now after 14 years working with libraries as well as having the experience of sitting on the board of a local charity I see the great value of volunteers in a nonprofit environment. Public libraries have deep experience on how to recruit, train, and manage volunteers. They are probably the most experienced group in the community on the subject.

In addition, using the community pyramid, the dashboard metrics, and the library website as a portal, the purpose-based library can be the focal point for connecting volunteers with good causes. The pyramid itself along with its dashboard metrics will not only inspire more volunteers, but also launch new programs to help build and repair the community.

Throughout this book we have proposed a great deal of work for the library and their staff, which is already stretched very thin. How can this already busy workforce support these additional requirements of the purpose-based library? Once again, they cannot do it alone, and they must recruit volunteers to help. Volunteers can support every effort we have presented. Imagine a future that not only has a Friends of the Library group, but a Friends of Child Literacy group, Friends of Adult Literacy group, Friends of the Community Safety Net group, and so on. The community library, however, must play a pivotal role in coordinating resources, building business networks, and providing meeting rooms and online training resources. These are activities in which libraries are highly skilled and experienced. In chapter 17 we will dive

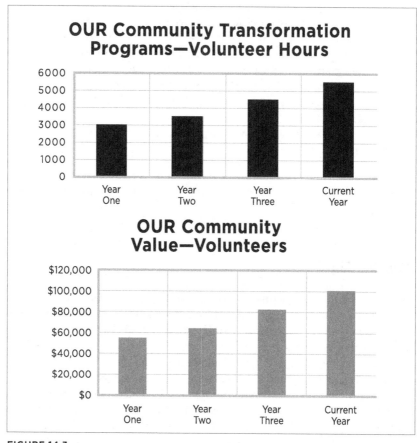

FIGURE 14.3
Community volunteers

more deeply into the issue of resource assignments, specifically the new role of the research/reference librarian.

We based our value assessment for community volunteers at $18 per hour as assessed by the Corporation of National and Community Service group.[6] Figure 14.3 shows dashboard metrics for community volunteers.

POTTER'S PERSPECTIVE, POINTS, AND PONDERINGS

In the past two chapters, we looked at the changing nature of labor. The "great recession" was cruel to many people in many ways. But two very interesting outcomes emerged during the time that the economy stabilized. First, there were lots of people looking for work, but there was a considerable gap between the skills of the unemployed and the skills desired by employers. Second, as the economy reset, the new normal appeared to be leaner and smaller. The end result is that there were fewer jobs and fewer matches between the skills in the market and the skills of the unemployed. As an employer, I saw this development. Although it was common to see 100 or more applications for our openings, frequently we could eliminate many from the field due to lack of skill or experience. In fact, during the height of the recession, we had to repost a system-wide youth services coordinator position three times in an attempt to build a strong enough pool with qualified applicants. Is this a once-in-a-generation problem, or is it the new normal?

I believe this could be the new normal mostly because change occurs so quickly. The idea that you can learn all you need for your career at one time is a very 20th century idea. The library can become the place where people can retrain and relearn with a fairly low entry threshold. Additionally, the idea that the best role for the library is to be a clearinghouse for job openings or a place for people to retool resumes is a 20th century library response. In the coming years, a relevant, successful, purpose-based library must provide assistance to people starting their own businesses, seeking to improve their skills, or desiring to acquire necessary vocational credentials.

Libraries that match interns with business internship programs and volunteers with volunteer programs build a stronger community. Libraries have a long history of being a landing place for volunteers; however, matching volunteer skills with volunteer needs will continue to be a challenge. In the coming years, library work will be more technical and require more specialized depth of knowledge. Additionally, there will be less shelving as more materials migrate to digital. Volunteer opportunities will still exist in libraries but not in the way we have seen in the past. Despite the challenge, these opportunities are important, as they can help connect people to their library. But with fewer books to shelve, fewer books libraries can purchase, and more hesitancy about adults working with children, we will have to be creative about how to best use volunteers to help fulfill our mission. The new normal will be our ability to help connect people with opportunities, whether they come with civic volunteerism or career and vocational development opportunities.

NOTES

1. Joe McKendrick, "New Role for Public Libraries: Small Business Incubators," SmartPlanet, *Bulletin* blog, February 19, 2013, www.smartplanet.com/blog/bulletin/new-role-for-public-libraries-small-business-incubators/13154.

2. Christina DesMarais, "16 Cool Coworking Spaces," *Inc.com*, www.inc.com/ss/christina-desmarais/16-cool-coworking-spaces.html.

3. "Our Efforts," Advocacy Resource Center of Macon, www.arcmacon.org/services/supported-employment.

4. Penny Loretto, "New Department of Labor Guidelines on Internships," About.com, Careers, http://internships.about.com/od/internships101/a/departmentoflaborsnewguidelinesforinterns.htm.

5. Jennifer Depaul, "The Real Cost of Long-Term Unemployment," *The Fiscal Times*, November 2, 2011, www.thefiscaltimes.com/Articles/2011/11/02/The-Real-Cost-of-Long-Term-Unemployment.

6. "Dollar Value of Volunteering for States," Corporation for National and Community Service, www.volunteeringinamerica.gov/pressroom/value_states.cfm.

15
Creative Expression

Above all, we are coming to understand that the arts incarnate the
creativity of a free people. When the creative impulse cannot flourish,
when it cannot freely select its methods and objects, when it is deprived
of spontaneity, then society severs the root of art.

—John F. Kennedy[1]

IN THIS CHAPTER WE PROPOSE THAT A COMMUNITY'S VITALITY is reflected in its expression of creativity and that creativity comes in many forms. We examine how libraries can become both enablers of creative members of the community and nurturers of an audience for their creative output. We present simple dashboard metrics to measure and market your progress.

I am either cursed or blessed as one of those people who have to be creative every day to feel alive. I totally understand the need and joy artists and musicians must feel when they embark on or complete a creative project. Unfortunately, I have little artistic talent and absolutely zero musical talent, but I do have a knack for creating new ideas and concepts. There are many in your community who feel this overriding desire to be creative but do not have the confidence, resources, or perhaps the audience to express their creative self. Satisfying this need brings us closer to the top of our pyramid at the Creative Expression step. Creativity is what holds our community together. It is what defines us as a community. Creativity launches new businesses, it entertains us, it inspires us, it gives a sense of worth, and most important, it provides a reason for us to gather as one. This is an exciting time for libraries, as many new ideas and concepts are tapping into the creative expression of their communities. Here are some great examples of new and creative concepts incubating at libraries across the country.

Chicago Public Library

Chicago Public Library is preparing to attract a wave of artisans, innovators, explorers and entrepreneurs through the doors of the Harold Washington Library Center with the addition of an Innovation Lab on its third floor. The Maker Lab is a cutting edge space for builders and creators complete with a variety of design software such as Trimble Sketchup, Inkscape, Meshlab, Makercam and equipment including three 3D Printers, two laser cutters, as well as a milling machine and vinyl cutter. The Maker Lab will serve to nurture experimentation, invention, exploration and Science, Technology, Engineering and Math (STEM) learning. The space offers something for every "maker" and "tinkerer" to explore.[2]

Chattanooga Public Library

Over four weeks in 2013, 10 teens will gather at the Chattanooga Public Library to record an album with Teen Librarian Justin Hoenke and local musicians who will serve as instructors. This multi-day participatory and hands-on learning experience will give teens ages 12-18 in the opportunity to gather at the library and create an album of original music.[3]

Skokie Public Library

A patron with no experience producing movies came to the Adult Services Computer Lab at Skokie Public Library, IL, requesting to use the Digital Media Lab. She wanted to scan images of her recently deceased uncle as part of a video memorial. She also wanted to use music (her uncle) wrote and recorded as the video's audio track.

A staff member began by teaching her how to use one of the lab's flatbed scanners—and the basics of Photoshop Elements 9—to digitize and enhance her images. Since she had nearly 100 images, a portable hard drive was checked out to her. At the next session, the patron was shown how to add the scanned images to an iMovie time line along with background music. Once all the images and music were added, she was shown how to put the credits at the beginning and end of the video and add statements to the images (such as dates, names of people in the pictures, and locations)—a considerable project—with staffers making suggestions throughout to help her realize her vision. Finally, the patron burned the movie to a DVD to show it to her family. It's all in a day's work for the Digital Media Lab.[4]

MID-CONTINENT PUBLIC LIBRARY

Libraries have always been in the literacy business. Too often, library literacy efforts begin and end with reading. In truth literacy is about reading, writing, listening, and the ability to share your thoughts. At a time when 140-character bursts of data pass for writing, the community needs more. Approaching literacy more holistically could be very beneficial. Building on a new strategic goal, MCPL started working to create the Story Center at Woodneath. The Story Center is a series of programs that help people develop their literacy skills. The staff at MCPL frequently say, "Everyone has a story in them, but not everyone is ready to tell that story." That's the focus of the Story Center. The library provides training classes, seminars, and peer groups for editing and improvement. Mid-Continent has also been collecting oral histories based on the NPR Story Corps model. This effort was initially centered around MCPL's extensive genealogy and family history program. However, it can also benefit people at the Story Center. These collections can serve as great source material for storytellers in all media. We will explore Mid-Continent's Story Center as a case study for self-publishing in chapter 21.

Providing resources is just one part of what libraries can do for their creative community members. They can also provide an audience. Libraries frequently display local artists' artwork in their lobby or in special rooms designed for this purpose. However, creativity goes beyond just expressions of art; it can also be expressions of interest. MCPL has built extensive display cases in their buildings and discovered that people are interested in sharing their personal collections with the larger community. For another example, Cloquet (MN) Public Library in the Arrowhead Library System has a display of dolls collected by a young girl born in the early 1900s who lived a brief and tender life. The display inspired the children's selector to write a story about the young girl's life based on the dolls displayed. We all know there are people who collect Coca-Cola items. How about a collection of lunch boxes, antique toys, or wherever your imagination takes you? What's fun about these displays is that you find some really interesting, passionate people in your community. You also unearth unknown treasures. Mid-Continent had a display on various artifacts that came from the Drumm Farm (a farm for orphaned children). The case was much commented on, created some community conversation, and helped build an even greater and engaged community.

These are great examples of a library partnership with creative members of the community. In the previous chapters we discussed establishing partnerships with local businesses to build and repair our community pyramid. Libraries can also be a link between the creative members of your community and local businesses. For example, a business could host an art competition and provide a space in their office to display the results; they could host lunchtime concerts, sponsor community theater events, or even evaluate an inventor's new product. Many airports I travel through display local artists' work. These partnerships may even lead to corporate sponsors for promising local talent. While libraries seek, engage, and transform their community, the community members respond by connecting, linking, understanding, and helping one another. Figure 15.1 shows dashboard metrics for creative arts. While we

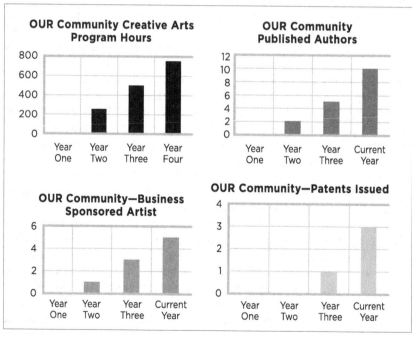

FIGURE 15.1
Creative arts

have not placed a value on these charts, I believe there are potential ways to place this value, such as tax income from new businesses in the creative field or the value earned from local patents. With a little creativity I believe your library can develop some meaningful valuations of your community's creative efforts.

POTTER'S PERSPECTIVE, POINTS, AND PONDERINGS

In this chapter we addressed an area where things are really changing for libraries. The historical role for a library is to collect content that someone else created and then to distribute that content. If you examined the collection found on a library's shelves 10 years ago, most (if not all) of the books would have been written by a professional author and made available through traditional publishers. It was up to the librarian to find the best quality and the most popular books, purchase them, and then circulate them to the community. The world is changing, and this is no longer the way that many books find their way to the library shelf. It is becoming more common for authors to have a much more direct hand in the publishing process. This isn't really vanity publishing. It is something different and frequently acts as an alternative with the fewer and fewer small presses.

I think that libraries have always been about collecting quality content. Is there any reason this shouldn't continue in the new environment? Interestingly, we always applied our quality check on the back end (after the item was published). In today's world, why can't the library help to assure quality earlier in the process? I think you can see from the examples in this chapter that there really is no reason why not.

It is important to understand that merely because people *can* create doesn't necessarily mean that they are *prepared* to create. Buying a 3-D printer and setting it up in your library really isn't good enough. Libraries need to help people understand good aesthetics and effective technique as well as technical expertise. This is a very appropriate role for libraries in the new century and the new economy.

In this chapter, we mentioned the idea of third-party displays, including an example from my library. I really like how libraries have started to make appeals to their communities to help create displays. Our library has encouraged people to bring in personal collections, self-created art, and other collections to display. We have discovered that people like to share their passions with the community. These displays make this possible and help connect the community. And they require very low-threshold service that can provide very high dividends within your community's pyramid.

NOTES

1. "John F. Kennedy on the Value of the Arts (archival)," http://newrealities.com/index.php/articles-on-creativity/item/900-john-f-kennedy-on-the-value-of-the-arts-archival?tmpl=component&print=1.
2. "Library Launches Maker Lab," *Bookmark*, Summer 2013, Chicago Public Library Foundation, http://www.cplfoundation.org/site/DocServer/Bookmark_Summer_2013_online-version.pdf?docID=342.
3. "Chattanooga Public Library Teen Music," Chattanooga Public Library, http://dml5.dmlcompetition.net/project/chattanooga-public-library-teen-music-lab.
4. "Build Your Own Digital Media Lab: Skokie Public Library's Media Lab," American Library Association, www.ala.org/transforminglibraries/build-your-own-digital-media-lab-skokie-public-library%E2%80%99s-media-lab.

16
Advancement of Knowledge

IN THIS CHAPTER WE PROPOSE THAT THE TRACKING AND COL-
lecting of community metrics is a form of organizational knowledge and
this concept is in tune with a key talent of librarians called knowledge organization. We discuss how libraries can become the center of organizational
knowledge for their community so the community (and the nation as a whole)
can learn from its successes and failures.

Years and years ago I was driving home from the airport when I had a
mind-blowing epiphany that hit me so hard I had to pull off the highway to
collect myself. My inspiration came from a common but frustrating phrase I
hear often from my clients: "We have tried that before." This often frustrates
me not only because it is an obstacle to change, but also because I want to
know more about what they actually had tried before. Why was it still not
in place? Did management not support it? Was it funded properly? Did they
pilot it? Did the pilot work? Did they establish metrics so we could evaluate
their results? Did it fail because there were no metrics? The idea was to create
a knowledge base of information that could be researched using key search
words, in other words, a project-based search engine (this was before there
were search engines). During my epiphany, I realized if we captured this organizational knowledge and created a search engine to access it, we could create
a learning organization.

Alas, I am not a cofounder of Google; however, with a much smaller purpose in mind, I followed up my idea by developing a software package called KnowledgeBase. The software allowed organizations to capture the experiences of a project team from infancy to completion and allow future project teams to search, study, and learn from past team's experiences. We had found a way for organizations to capture their collective knowledge and then advance that knowledge using simple search tools. In other words, those who do not know their history lose a great opportunity to advance beyond their past. My software was obsolete long ago, but the concept lives on, specifically in an online software tool I use called Smartsheet (go to www.smartsheet .com for more information). Today this concept is referred to as organizational knowledge and organizational learning.

There was a time when libraries were the only source available to advance one's knowledge, especially if one could not afford books. That time has passed.

However, while I was researching the current state of organizational knowledge, Google switched my search term from "organizational knowledge" to "knowledge organization." I was curious so I clicked on the "Knowledge organization" Wikipedia article. Here is what I found.

> The term knowledge organization (KO) (or "organization of knowledge," "organization of information" or "information organization") designates a field of study related to *Library and Information Science (LIS)*. In this meaning, KO is about activities such as document description, indexing and classification performed in libraries, databases, archives, and so on. These activities are done by librarians, archivists, and subject specialists as well as by computer algorithms.[1]

I had to laugh. Steve and I are proposing that librarians take on the new role of documenting, indexing, and classifying the dashboard metrics and their community's accomplishments to create a KnowledgeBase pyramid for their community. Apparently this is nothing new to librarians. Whether it is called knowledge organization or organizational knowledge we still find ourselves in the world of librarians. Librarians have the tools, the education, and the skills to support the advancement of organizational (community) knowledge and organizational (community) learning.

COMMUNITY LEARNING

With the Advancement of Knowledge (Community Learning) step, we have reached near the top of our pyramid. For any individual or organization to reach their full potential, they must constantly advance their knowledge base. As implied in the prior section, we are not just talking about the knowledge advancement of individuals, but also the knowledge advancement of the community as a whole.

There are two components of community learning:

Historical knowledge—learning from the past so your community can improve upon your future

Shared knowledge—understanding, examining, and incorporating new ideas to influence the future

Historical Knowledge

Throughout this book we have established dashboard metrics on the health of our community pyramid. If this concept is embraced, in a few years your library system will have established a history of knowledge-based metrics on the health and well-being of your community. If it is done properly, your community will also know what actions were taken to affect your pyramid as well as what worked and what did not. This constitutes the advancement of community knowledge from a historical basis.

Librarians are well positioned and well suited to archive and share the dashboard metrics and the programs behind them. The purpose-based library would combine their skills in preserving historical information as well as their abilities to document, index, and classify information and create an extremely valuable knowledge base for their community. The community will be able to tie specific cause-and-effect actions to the health of their pyramid, and the community can properly respond with this advanced knowledge.

Shared Knowledge

Historical knowledge allows us to learn from the past, but it does not provide new and creative ideas to advance beyond this past. Libraries already host educational and topical speakers and events. We propose these speakers and programs become aligned with the steps of the pyramid. In addition to invited speakers, there is a wealth of information on the internet to help educate and guide your community. In chapter 13, we discussed a new library website with a portal for every step of the community pyramid. At this site a member of the community could click on one of the pyramid steps, see the dashboard metrics, and find opportunities to help as well as be guided to books, webinars, speeches, and research articles on the topic. For example, TED Talks is a terrific resource for tapping into current research and new ideas on social issues. TED is a global set of conferences sponsored and owned by the nonprofit Sapling Foundation, under the slogan "Ideas worth spreading." You can download any of the more than 1,500 TED talks free online or from a paid service provider such as Netflix. The main categories to choose from include technology, entertainment, design, business, science, and global issues. The speakers are typically experts in their field, and talks range from 10 to 20 minutes. I have been exposed to topics I could never have imagined and amazingly enough can apply to my everyday life and business. For example, one talk was about how to solve traffic jams in Switzerland. I found it fascinating, and I discovered new ideas I can use to streamline business processes. Libraries are well positioned to assist their communities in becoming learning communities. After all, that is what libraries were meant to do.

POTTER'S PERSPECTIVE, POINTS, AND PONDERINGS

The collection and dissemination of knowledge are what libraries do. Libraries have already lost to Google and Wikipedia for surface web data. That's not what we are talking about here. The best way I can describe it is the same way I used to describe it when I taught in library school.

Data are individual pieces of information that are fairly objective. Information becomes more useful as interpretations and conclusions are drawn from several pieces of data. Then, as the information becomes more useful, and sometimes more widely accepted, it becomes wisdom. Let's take a piece of data as a stock price for HuberCorp at 45 3/8. This is data because it tells us something about the value of HuberCorp. Is this good or bad data? Is the information useful? What does it mean to me if I know virtually nothing about the stock market? Interestingly, this is the type of content that is fairly easy to find in Google.

Next we have information. This is when we take our data from HuberCorp and compare it over the past two weeks and discover that 14 days ago it was sitting at 5 1/2. We keep looking and discover that the CEO, John Huber, is about to release a groundbreaking book, and anticipation is driving the price up. So, knowing that in two weeks the stock rose about 40 points in value means something. Merely knowing that the stock is sitting at 45 3/8 really doesn't mean anything. This is still fairly easy to find online and in resources other than libraries.

However, it is when you get to knowledge or wisdom that you really have something. In our example, we now have rating services and other well-respected experts in the field writing reports and creating a conventional wisdom that HuberCorp is the next great stock boom. Where are you going to find that kind of analysis? This is where libraries clearly come in. The evaluation of the quality of knowledge and wisdom as it migrates from information takes a human. It takes a librarian. Additionally, quality information is costly and frequently more expensive for the average individual consumer to afford to purchase. Gathering the resources of the community to create an economy of scale is what libraries do. I agree that the daily stock prices are easy to get online at CBS Marketwatch or any number of online sites. Libraries can't and shouldn't compete there. Even some basic trending is easy to get online and for no charge. However, the true analysis, the consideration of the company's strength and long-term implications, has real value.

The move from information to knowledge is an arena where libraries still can compete and lead the way. Libraries can allow citizens to band together to buy access to knowledge and to have that knowledge available for the whole community. This helps to assure fair market conditions, equal opportunity in schools, and for the purposes of this book, wisdom to rebuild a community.

NOTE

1. "Knowledge organization," *Wikipedia*, http://en.wikipedia.org/wiki/ Knowledge_organization.

PART III

Growth

In part I, we addressed survival by embracing the concepts and tools of Lean Library Management. In part II, we unveiled the community pyramid and a purpose-based road map of community engagement and community organizational knowledge to differentiate libraries from Google, Amazon, and Netflix. While this purpose-based approach provides a path toward success, growth hinges on how libraries use this path to their competitive advantage.

We believe growth depends on the following key factors:

- Available and properly aligned resources
- Value-added marketing and metrics
- Increased funding
- Increased market share through new and innovative services and product offerings
- Leveraging buying power
- Passionate supporters

In part III, Steve and I will provide our perspective on this road map to growth. However, it is not our intent to make this a one-way highway of answers. It is our purpose to get the discussion going, as there are many other roads that are traveling in the same direction. What is important is that libraries as a whole have the same destination in mind.

17
Resources

I N THIS CHAPTER WE PROPOSE THAT THE CURRENT APPROACH to staffing a library is not always in tune with the purpose-based library. We also discuss how critical skills in the library are being underutilized or eliminated altogether. We suggest how these skills can be repurposed toward facilitating the competitive differentiation of libraries as well as the improvement of the community's pyramid health and well-being.

In the previous chapters we called for librarians to create, collect, collate, organize, and present their local community's dashboard metrics. We proposed that the community library be a focal point for businesses, neighborhoods, charities, and government programs to repair, rebuild, and improve their pyramid. We called for libraries to embrace their mission and their purpose to seek, engage, and transform. But who is going to do it?

A few months ago I was asked to apply my Lean Library Methodology to a large urban central library. As my lean methodology directs, we formed a cross-functional team and set out to identify all the service delivery chains the central library supported. A very important lean tool I use is called the Pareto principle. Vilfredo Pareto was an Italian engineer, sociologist, economist, and political scientist at the turn of the 20th century who observed that 80 percent of the wealth was held by 20 percent of the people. As it turned out,

Pareto's 80/20 rule applies to just about any topic. For example, 80 percent of complaints come from 20 percent of the customers, and for our discussion in this chapter, 80 percent of staff time is consumed by 20 percent of the tasks. As a consultant I get the most bang for the buck by focusing on the 20 percent that affect the 80 percent. Our cross-functional team used a lean tool I call transactional cost analysis to uncover the 20 percent. All staff members identified the tasks they worked on each week as well as provided an estimate of the time they spent on each task. It was not intended to be perfect but to give us a ballpark direction for finding our 20 percent. Our grouping fell along the lines of circulation, reference, business support, children's, and A/V. For our purposes, we will focus our discussion on circulation and reference. Our transaction analysis survey results are in the chart in figure 17.1.

The analysis revealed that nearly 50 percent of staff time in the circulation service delivery chain is dedicated to managing customer accounts. We applied the 80/20 rule to understand which tasks consumed the most time within this 20 percent. The results are shown in table 17.1.

During the project we also applied the 80/20 rule to the reference support staff service delivery chain. The reference group's 80/20 results are shown in figure 17.2.

The chart revealed the reference staff spends most of their time providing technical assistance to users of the public computer. Table 17.2 dives deeper into the technical assistance category.

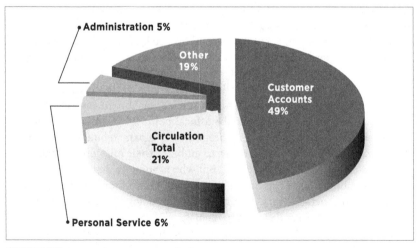

FIGURE 17.1
Circulation Pareto analysis

TABLE 17.1
Circulation customer account support 80/20

SDC Category	Total Staff Hours	Percent of Total	Cumulative Percent of Total
Create/modify library accounts (in person)	34.00	31%	31%
E-mail	26.00	24%	55%
Answer other account questions	13.00	12%	67%
Collections issues	13.00	12%	79%
Online card apps	10.50	10%	89%
Paying fines in person	4.00	4%	92%
Proofreading card apps	4.00	4%	96%
Bounced e-mail account maintenance	2.00	2%	98%
Phone account questions	1.25	1%	99%
Change of address	1.00	1%	100%
TOTAL	**108.75**	**100%**	

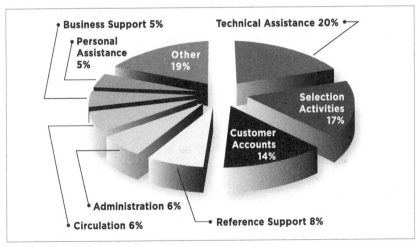

FIGURE 17.2
Reference support staff Pareto analysis

TABLE 17.2

Reference staff technical support Pareto analysis

SDC Category	Total Staff Hours	Percent of Total	Cumulative Percent of Total
PC customer assistance	18.00	26%	26%
Printing from PC assistance	12.70	18%	45%
Collect money for ear buds/mf prints	6.10	9%	54%
Assist customers with photocopiers	5.60	8%	62%
Place customer photocopy requests	5.35	8%	69%
Monitor queue area	4.30	6%	76%
Clean public computers	3.55	5%	81%
Make change for photocopiers	3.55	5%	86%
Reprint customer job files	3.15	5%	91%
Change printer cartridges	1.85	3%	93%
Investigate customer complaints/ problems	1.70	2%	96%
Refill paper in printers and photocopiers	0.55	1%	97%
Adding credit accounts/printing	0.52	1%	97%
Computer/printer maintenance	0.50	1%	98%
Maintain copy & shredder machines	0.50	1%	99%
Printing from PC assistance—GRR	0.33	0%	99%
Collect money from copiers and prepare bags for bank	0.25	0%	100%
Take monthly counts for copiers and send report to Fotos	0.25	0%	100%
TOTAL	**68.75**	**100%**	

The conclusion by the team and the management staff was that the circulation staff spent most of their time managing customer account paperwork while the reference staff's time (some of the library's most educated, trained, experienced, and I might add, well-paid staff members) was consumed by tasks that a high school graduate could support.

To survive you must create a more flexible and responsive organization with a crew aligned to leverage your competitive advantages. The lesson of the

Pareto principle is that you can make a larger and more leveraged impact on reducing costs and freeing up valuable staff time by streamlining those few tasks that consume the most time. Lean and the Pareto principle will help you design this more flexible, realigned, and responsive organization. However, the best organizations do not just initiate across-the-board staff cuts. They retain and redirect their best staff members to pursue even more lean improvements as well as to add new and improved products and services for their customers. This assures success and growth. This is the direction we believe libraries must follow. Streamline, improve, and realign core services to free up the best staff members so they can be redirected to an innovative path of success and growth.

We are concerned that due to the budget issues of the current and future economy, libraries are losing some of their most valuable resources. We are specifically concerned for the fate of the research/reference librarian. Every library knows that Google has changed the role of reference staff. Figure 17.2 attests to this fact, as only eight percent of the reference staff's time in this case study is spent on reference activities. Most public libraries recognize that their reference staff is being underutilized. Some public libraries have eliminated the position altogether. We believe this is a mistake. The purpose-based library would redirect these resources to pursue the ideas and concepts of this book. The enlightened library leadership teams and their library boards would look beyond budget cuts toward a path of success and growth. This path of success and growth will need the best, brightest, and most experienced librarians as a resource. These communities must see the value libraries provide and be willing to not only keep funding libraries, but also increase the funding for the value-added services they provide. This is where the purpose-based library shines.

POTTER'S PERSPECTIVE, POINTS, AND PONDERINGS

Our profession has experienced dramatic change over the past 25 years. Automation and technology have changed the way that we receive information, the way that information is gathered, and the way it is distributed. Additionally, automation and technology have changed the way libraries operate and have redefined the skill sets we require.

When I started working at Mid-Continent Public Library, we still had a paper card catalog and we still circulated our materials using the Gaylord Charging Machine. Library work was very labor intensive. A catalog card had to be created for every author, title, or subject. Library staff had to file those cards and constantly update the catalog. For interlibrary loan, if you didn't know the title, staff had to search through volumes of *Books in Print*. Once a patron found a book to check out, it would be linked to his or her account by embossing the user ID number to a paper card. That card would be manually filed. When you returned the item, that card would have to be retrieved, matched back with the book, and then the item could be reshelved. Patrons were highly dependent on library staff. Today online catalogs and self-service checkout allows a totally customer-driven experience with little need of a library staff member.

Research was also labor intensive and skill based. Because it was hard to retrieve information, libraries trained people to find obscure facts. We had our favorite go-to sources. I always believed that if I had the *World Book*, *Statistical Abstract of the United States*, *Sears Subject Headings* book, and any general-purpose almanac, I could have a fighting chance on the reference desk. Today, the least sophisticated searcher can pull the obscure facts I trained years to find by doing a simple Google search. We have to accept that we are no longer the finders of obscure data. Everyone can do that.

We must accept the fact that the public we serve no longer places value on many of the professional skills and values we offer. Does the average user care that Wikipedia articles are generally less researched than *World Book*? No. The average user wants an answer immediately, and wants it to be "good enough." It doesn't have to be perfect. And because these sources are often as easy to access as one's pocket (on a smartphone) we can't compete for ease. We lost to Google and Wikipedia for surface web answers. We need to wave the white flag and find what we can do that these omnipresent resources cannot.

Where does that leave libraries? If we are willing to rethink ourselves, we can repurpose our current skill set in new and creative ways. Mid-Continent is already on this path. However, and surprising to many people, MCPL never supported a classic reference department like other libraries of our size. If we had, it would have been a logical step to repurpose our reference librarians in this new direction, but because we could not do this, we hired a statistical analyst to meet the same need. Her addition to our team has been incredible. One day I was thinking about creating an educational partnership like Los Angeles Public Library, as John outlined in chapter 13. I figured the first step would be to determine where to implement the partnership. If we could determine the census tracts (and correlated branch service areas) with the highest number of adults with less than a high school diploma, we could focus our effort. The statistical analyst came back with a list of 10 census tracts for me to choose where we could launch our service. This helped me to identify what community partners to approach and how to move forward with this kind of partnership. Using *DemographicsNow*, *ReferenceUSA*, *American FactFinder* and other US Census data, a good reference librarian could do the same thing.

The purpose-based library must recognize that streamlining their operations, moving to more self-service transactions, and migrating to e-books will free up a large part of their staff. These freed-up staff members can become your resources to seek, engage, and transform your community pyramid. This path takes your library beyond survival, beyond success, to growth.

Unfortunately, library staff, library administrators, and library boards often think about streamlined processes as a way to cut jobs and save money. Sometimes you are forced to do that. But the fact of the matter is that streamlining to recapture and reallocate is what makes sense.

At MCPL we developed a concept called the Customer-Centered Transaction Model (CCTM). I actually started down this road so we could call our self-service options something other than "self-service." What we discovered is that if you put your customer in the center of the transaction, you provide service in a way that the customer wants it. The opposite of customer-centered would be staff-centered. That's something that we all know far too well. We have storytime at 10 a.m. because that works best for our scheduling. We keep the holds behind the circulation desk because it is handy for the staff. But what if you start asking what is handy for the customer? This is CCTM.

What does CCTM look like? Long before CCTM, we migrated to a system that allowed our customers to manage their printing and control their internet access. We even allowed adults to filter or unfilter their internet access without staff mediation. There was no need for us to manage these transactions. Customers seemed willing and able. Next, we employed a self-service holds system driven by John Huber's Lean "One and Done" Holds Label System. We discovered that people didn't mind pulling their own holds. In fact, it allowed many to come in, get the item, and check it out at a self-check terminal in no time.

We explored other options that put the customer in the center of the transaction instead of the staff. We migrated our summer reading program registration to a website where customers enroll themselves. No more registration index cards filled out by staff. But the real big move has been to flip our ratio of circulation terminals and self-check machines. If a library had four circulation transaction terminals and two self-checks, we would change that to four self-checks and two circulation terminals. One important part of this migration is to include as many stations as possible where a customer can pay fines without staff mediation.

Some may be concerned that a customer-driven transaction actually takes the customer longer than a staff-assisted transaction. Perhaps, but during a preconference at PLA in Boston (2006), I learned that when people are in control of their own transactions, they routinely feel that it is more convenient, even if it takes longer. You know this to be true. When was the last time you used a bank teller when an ATM was available? Do you use a travel agent or a travel website like Travelocity or Expedia?

Our branches that use CCTM now see between 80 to 85 percent of their transactions unmediated by our staff. What does that mean for library staff?

At MCPL, it means that we can have fewer people chained to the circulation desk. Fewer people tied up at the circulation desk means more of our staff can interact with customers in the stacks and at the computers, which allows us to have more meaningful conversations and relationships with our customers while not tying up the transaction counter. CCTM allows us time to seek, engage, and transform.

Even more important, CCTM allows us to go outside our building. Many of our community members do not have the mobility required to fully use the library and their services. Many kids are confined to a day care, where they cannot afford the cost of transporting these children to the library's 10 a.m. storytime. Have you visited a Walmart at 10 p.m. on a school night? You see families everywhere. It is not always by choice, as some parents are working two jobs and 10 p.m. is the only time they can grocery shop. This family will find it hard to schedule a time to go to the library. CCTM frees up resources so you can provide literacy-based storytimes not only at day care centers but (yes, I said it) at Walmart.

To be relevant, a library has to be a place and a service at the same time. Ultimately, I believe a library has to be about access. If you can best provide access to a service in your building, that's great. If you can provide access to a service outside your building, that's great too. But the fact is, you have to do both, and I don't think you can do both without figuring out a new way to reallocate resources. CCTM and lean do that.

18
Value-Added Marketing

DURING MY WORKSHOPS I OFTEN COMPARE LIBRARIES TO A manufacturing operation. Libraries have a research/development group (collection development), a manufacturing group (technical services), a distribution group (delivery), and a retail group (circulation). However, in contrast to my manufacturing clients, there is one group that is often not represented: marketing. Libraries are quick to admit that they do a poor job marketing their services. Marketing is more than just getting the word out about what value-added services you provide. Marketing is convincing the customers that they cannot live without the product or service you offer. Huber's hierarchy of community needs provides a tangible and presentable definition of what a community needs to be healthy and how a library services those needs. It provides the framework to show the tangible impact your library is having on your community. Every person who lives in a community will understand what the pyramid represents, not only for them personally but for their kids, for their friends, and for their neighbors. However, the pyramid alone will not accomplish this, for without metrics, it is hollow, useless. With the pyramid, combined with the metrics, libraries have the means to not only define and measure the health of their community, but also to actively market how they impact these metrics. In the future, when a community member is asked what the library does, the answer will be "They build and support our community's health and well-being, and we can't do without them."

In this chapter we propose that community-based dashboard metrics and community partnerships can frame and feed an effective marketing strategy leading to growth and increased library funding.

During a delivery service improvement team meeting at Austin Public Library, I took the opportunity to present an overview of the purpose-based library, the pyramid, and the dashboard metrics. I asked the group for marketing ideas to engage the community in these transformation efforts, as this is the key to success. One of the team members weighed in: "I feel that we too often preach to the choir. We do a good job marketing our website, newsletters, and so on to our current customers, but we could do a much better job reaching out to those in the community that do not use the library or are not aware of what the library offers."

She has a good point. To fully engage the community, the purpose-based library should leverage their current patron base but also go outside their four walls to engage the rest of the community. To do so, the purpose-based library needs a marketing strategy.

We propose the following steps to create your strategy.

Step 1: Define your desired marketing outcomes

Step 2: Develop a positive, consistent, concise, and proactive brand message

Step 3: Understand your market needs

Step 4: Define your market segments

Step 5: Establish your marketing targets

Step 6: Establish a marketing budget

Step 7: Change the conversation with value-based dashboard metrics

Step 8: Create portals of education, communication, and connection

Step 9: Celebrate

Step 10: Create a 100-year Truth and Values Plan

STEP 1
DEFINE YOUR DESIRED MARKETING OUTCOMES

Any good plan begins at the end. What is it we want to accomplish? What do we want the world to look like as a result of these efforts? How do we want people to respond? For libraries, the ultimate objective is to have a community dedicated to transforming the health of their pyramid. Libraries want to be seen as a focal point for this effort. Not only do they want people to recognize the true value a community receives by investing in their local library, they want these investments to be celebrated. They want to change the conversation from libraries as book lenders to libraries as an effective value-added resource for community transformation. These objectives should drive your marketing plan. Once again, if you do not measure it, it must not be important. You should begin by establishing your specific and measurable marketing objectives, such as:

- By the end of the fiscal year recruit 100 new library advocates to engage in our community and spread the branding message that libraries provide value-added services to the community.
- By the end of the fiscal year recruit 20 new business partnerships and engage these partners to develop strategies to transform the community pyramid.
- By the end of the fiscal year create 20 new physical locations to advertise the library's brand message.
- By the end of the fiscal year create a series of 25 published stories highlighting the impact libraries have had on their community members.
- By the end of the fiscal year increase traffic to the library's community transformation website by 30 percent.
- For each quarter, host an event to celebrate the accomplishments of the library's community and business advocates.
- By the end of the fiscal year increase library funding for community transformation events by 25 percent.

Your marketing goals should define a specific time frame and specific metrics to measure success. While these metrics are separate from your community pyramid dashboard metrics, you could certainly create dashboard metrics to track your progress.

STEP 2
DEVELOP A POSITIVE, CONSISTENT, CONCISE, AND PROACTIVE BRAND MESSAGE

First, one lesson I have learned as an agent of change is that you cannot sell the negative. Negative messages, negative voices, and negative advertising motivate and convince no one. The objective of a library marketing strategy is to get people excited about the library and to speak positively about what libraries are accomplishing in the community. However, the message that our community pyramid is broken and needs to be fixed is purely negative. It may be true that it is broken, but this message is not the way to motivate people to action. They must be inspired, and inspiration comes from positive thoughts, emotions, and inner purpose. Therefore, your brand message must be positive.

Second, the brand message must leverage libraries' most important competitive advantages, your national footprint and your local community knowledge. Organizations like ALA, PLA, or your state association should leverage your national footprint by creating campaigns for libraries throughout a region or throughout the nation. But a national message will only take you so far. Your brand must speak to your audience. You need to utilize the broad national footprint of libraries and leverage this broad platform, but you also need to create a message that speaks to your community.

Third, the brand message must be concise and reflect the true value to the community.

Every successful brand message is short, succinct, catchy, and memorable. "Have it your way," "I'm lovin' it," "Things go better with Coke," "Be a Pepper," and "JUST DO IT" are each examples of concise and memorable brand messages that reflect the company's desired image. Libraries today do have a consistent image, and it tends to focus on books and reading. A brief surface web search for posters and slogans for libraries produced the following:

- "Don't Buy, Borrow"
- "Look, It's Books."
- "You Could Be Reading"
- "READ"
- "I Love Libraries"

My favorite, of course, is "I Love Libraries," but even that message does not express the value-added nature of libraries and how they impact the community where your patrons live. Most of these branding messages feed the image that libraries only do one thing—books. A better branding message would emphasize value, service, transformation, and community. Here are a few of my ideas:

- "Libraries, A Community Transformation at Work"
- "Libraries, The Future Created by You"
- "Libraries, A Million Stories, A Million Successes"
- "Libraries, A Billion Words to Build Upon"
- "Libraries, Where Ideas Begin"

And my favorite, said with a whisper:

- "Sshhhh, can you hear the library working?"

I am sure there are many other good ideas out there to express the true value of libraries.

Finally, the brand message must be proactive. Libraries can no longer sit on the sidelines and allow others to define them. Libraries most become proactive in having their voice heard and their value understood. With local community knowledge and more physical locations than any other business in North America (plus having a huge bank of email addresses), the possibilities are limitless.

STEP 3
UNDERSTAND YOUR MARKET NEEDS

Under our current environment, most libraries define the typical patron's needs as follows:

> Our patrons want to self-pickup and self-checkout their books after they are delivered within 24 hours of availability to the library of their choice.

The current national conversation about the long-term viability of libraries tells me that members of your community want more from their local library than just self-serviced books. All community members desire to live in a safe, healthy, and thriving community; however, they may not be aware that there is a powerful tool out there already helping them. Libraries can no longer wait to be discovered—they must get out into the community and show their value. If their community is presented back to them in a way that they can see where help is needed, they will look for those who provide answers. Currently those who shout the loudest get the most attention. Libraries do not need to have the loudest voice because a calm and confident voice that leads and shows results is more effective than a loud voice that does not. With the pyramid, libraries have the ability to be the facilitator who leads with a calm and confident voice. Sshhhh, can you hear the library working?

STEP 4
DEFINE YOUR MARKET SEGMENTS

Once libraries have their goals, brand message, and common voice, your team must determine who should hear the message. From my experience, libraries see the world similarly to how they organize their books. They see the world as, for example:

- Juvenile readers
- Young Adult readers
- Nonfiction readers
- Popular Fiction readers
- Romance readers
- Western readers
- Science Fiction/Fantasy readers

This view of your market might identify reader groups and existing customers, but it does not provide you the best means to find those in the community in need of assistance or find those resources in the community to help. This will be the key to successful community transformation.

While developing your market segments, keep in mind your purpose and your pyramid. Your branches intuitively know which steps in the pyramid are in most need in their community, and as you collect your dashboard metrics you will reinforce or perhaps change these perceptions. Allow this to drive your market segments, and adapt as needed. Example market segments might include literacy at-risk adults, literacy at-risk third graders, diabetes at-risk communities, home invasion at-risk neighborhoods, at-risk student dropouts, at-risk socially isolated communities, communities without creative tools and resources, at-risk single working mothers, at-risk digital literacy neighborhoods, lack of computers and high-speed-internet neighborhoods, and so on. This defines our target market of those in need, but we also need target markets of those who can help. This includes businesses, volunteers, and philanthropic resources. Example market segments might include businesses in the creative market, businesses with statistical analytical skills, businesses with a history of community engagement, business with a large number of employees, businesses with large job postings, businesses with entry-level jobs, and so on. For volunteers you might define your market segments as retired businessmen and women, senior citizens, past library volunteers, community college students, high school students, and last but not least, church members.

We cannot of course forget your current customer base supported by your primary lending functions. As Steve indicated, OrangeBoy has created some great tools to define your markets and you have a wealth of data sitting in your ILS. Table 18.1 provides a first-cut definition of your current patron market segments.

TABLE 18.1

Library usage

Customer Category	Total Population	Percent of Total
	622,400	
Cardholders	415,500	67%
Volunteers	968	0.16%
Fanatic Users	45,705	11%
Frequent Users	319,935	77%
Infrequent Users	50,691	12%
Not a Card Owner	206,900	33%

TABLE 18.2

Businesses by sample ZIP code, US Census

Industry Code	Description	Total	20-49	50-99	100-249	250-499	500-999
21	Oil and Gas	57	2	2	2	0	0
22	Utilities	4	1	1	1	0	0
23	Construction	35	1	1	0	0	1
31	Manufacturing	8	2	0	2	0	1
42	Wholesale Trade	47	2	1	1	0	0
44	Retail Trade	52	7	1	0	0	0
48	Trans/ Warehousing	9	0	1	0	0	0
51	Information	25	2	3	1	0	0
52	Finance and Insurance	165	13	3	1	0	0
53	Real Estate	68	1	0	2	0	0
54	Professional/Tech Services	193	11	4	0	1	0
55	Management Enterprises	24	4	4	2	0	0
56	Adm, Waste, Remediation	75	7	4	5	1	2
61	Educational Services	9	1	0	1	0	0
62	Health Care and Social Assist	298	24	10	9	4	0
71	Arts, Enter. Recreation	11	1	1	1	0	0
72	Accommodation/ Food Services	55	16	3	2	0	0
81	Other	80	5	1	1	0	1
	Total	**1,215**	**100**	**40**	**31**	**6**	**5**

Once again, research/reference librarians are trained and skilled to find information. They should be more than qualified to research and define these market segments. The US Census Bureau, the CDC, and DemographicsNow are a few examples of sites that can be a resource. I am sure your research/reference librarians know of many more.

For example, table 18.2 provides a basic breakdown of businesses for one particular zip code surrounding a branch library. This data was easily obtained through the US Census Bureau.[1]

As you develop more detailed marketing segments (including driving your usage numbers to the branch level) you can further tailor your strategy.

STEP 5
ESTABLISH YOUR MARKETING TARGETS

You have your objective, your brand message, and your audience. Now you need an approach. It is beyond the scope of this book to develop a targeted marketing campaign for each market segment you define; however, we can establish some guidelines and sprinkle in a few ideas along the way. We encourage you to brainstorm your own unique approach tailored to your community needs and resources.

The Helpers

Libraries need agents of change, a group of thinking partners who understand the value of libraries and are invested in the library's success. We are not talking about typical volunteers who run the annual book sale or help shelve books. We are talking about a different type of volunteer who is neither "friend" nor "foundation." These volunteers are advocates to help change the conversation. Your fanatic users and frequent users groups might be an excellent place to start recruiting your agents of change. Create a special Gold library club card for these fanatic users and a Silver club card for the frequent users. Host Gold-members-only events and Silver-members-only events. Have a special club newsletter that provides talking points on how they can promote the library at social gatherings as well as online social sites. In their special newsletter provide them inspiring stories of community transformation that they can share. Stories about the "at risk" child who learned to love to read because of storytime, the adult who could not read English who is now reading the *First American, The Life and Times of Benjamin Franklin*, the high school dropout who acquired her high school diploma from the library, the grandma who talked to her grandchild through the internet for the first time, or the homeless person who found a home. The stories are endless, and they happen at libraries every day. Give them statistics from your community pyramid and give them a behind-the-scenes look at what is happening at the library.

Through these efforts, find those select few who will go that extra mile to promote the library throughout the community. From this group also find those special people who will lead and assist in community transformation efforts. For those who volunteer, create a Signature club, where they are recognized with their signatures and pictures on the library walls. With permission, put them on your website, get their pictures in the local newspapers. To transform your community you must have an army of change agents. Start with those who love the library the most. If you provide them the opportunity to make a difference, many will respond with enthusiasm.

Go outside your walls and prove to your community businesses that libraries have services that will benefit their organization. Expose them to your services, your educational resources, your marketing data, your trade magazines, your sample business plans, and your on-site meeting resources. As Steve says, if you first ask what the library can do for them, it is much easier to ask what they can do for their community.

An effective marketing effort lives where your target market lives. Amazon .com has established partnerships with libraries where library websites will link a customer to Amazon.com to buy a book they could not find at the library. (I will hold my tongue on my opinion of whether this is a good idea or not for libraries, but if you read *Lean Library Management*, you know how I feel.) Amazon provides a perfect example of living where your customer lives—libraries! I would advise libraries to ask Amazon to reciprocate this deal and place library brand messaging on their website in exchange. As Amazon shows us, nearly everyone lives on the internet and social media these days, and therefore libraries must have a presence there as well. The advertising noise on the internet is becoming just that—noise—so libraries must be clever about how they establish this presence. Seek out and engage those markets through social media, and target those who can provide help in your transformation efforts. We cannot ignore how Facebook, Twitter, and the rest have changed our lives. There is a reason Facebook posted record profits of $1.8 billion in the second quarter of 2014. How many times do you check your favorite social media site each day? However, once again, libraries must cut through the noise. By creating short, heartrending stories with a catchy picture about individuals in their local community whose lives have changed because of the library will not only cut through the noise, it will change the conversation.

Social networking can serve as a surrogate for the type of interaction that you find in traditional networking. For example, you can create robust online interaction by posting a question like "What are you reading this weekend?" or "What books have you abandoned?" It is surprising where a simple question like this can take you. It is important to use social networking tools as they are designed and not just as a way to drive people to your website. For instance, use Twitter to give people up-to-the-minute updates on an event like the Summer Reading Kick-Off Carnival or upload pictures in real time for events like grand openings. Use Pinterest to display DIY programs or art that was created in the library. Mid-Continent Public Library actually cross-links library blog posts with Facebook posts to make sure the message is seen. Interestingly, more conversation and dialogue typically occurs within the social networking sites and not on the library's blogs. Creating posts like "The 15 Authors to 'Like' on Facebook" or "10 Books to Read Before You See the Movie" will be a great conversation starter. It is important to be very intentional about social networking efforts.

Once you have established a relationship with these businesses and organizations, recruit those special groups that not only understand that a strong community is in their best interests, but also are motivated to help. Just as we did for your fanatic users, create a Signature business club. Provide these groups their own quarterly newsletter with talking points and community transformation stories. Create a wall that displays your Signature-awarded businesses. List their accomplishments on your website and promote their stories in the local newspaper. Provide them a plaque to hang on their wall celebrating their accomplishments. Hold special events and invite all the businesses in the area to attend. For your Signature business members, have a special on-site summertime lunch storytime event for the children of their employees (with adults invited), bring in people who can tell stories on how the library changed their lives, and end the event with an informal and fun-based "idea generation" exercise. Do the same with nonprofit organizations and clubs in your community.

I discovered a great example of this over dinner one night with the director and assistant director of the Austin Public Library, Brenda Branch and Toni Lambert. They shared a story about a partnership they had established with

a self proclaimed "NERD" group in Austin. They sent me this Whispers newsletter from *The Fact Daily*, an online subscription-based political newspaper.

> Self-described nerd J. C. Dwyer and 900 other citizens have signed a
> petition urging the City Council to put more funding into Austin's librar-
> ies this year. Dwyer says he and others have had productive conver-
> sations with several members of Council and their staff and feels they
> have a good chance to increase the limited funds that caused libraries
> to cut their hours several years ago. "They run a pretty tight ship," he
> said. "They just barely have enough resources to do their job."
>
> In addition to the petition, Dwyer's group has sponsored a letter
> writing campaign, which produced a multitude of hand-written letters,
> including some from children to get the Council's attention.[2]

Perhaps there are J. C. Dwyers and a NERD group in your community as well.

Those in Need

We have given examples throughout this book on how to find and engage
those in need in your community. We rely heavily on the school librarian to
identify at-risk third graders, we rely on branch staff to identify at-risk adults
in literacy, homelessness, and digital literacy. Our marketing approach for
those in need relies heavily on customer engagement, which creates the competitive differentiation we seek. This will require some changes in your staffing and training. You will need to train your staff to not only assist, but to
engage. You will need to free up your staff from supporting transactions to
supporting face-to-face engagement. I do not think brochures and physical
marketing tools will help engage literacy-related at-risk children and adults
or motivate the homeless to seek help. However, other areas of the pyramid
such as Creative Expression, Social Community Engagement, Advancement
of Knowledge, and Digital Literacy and Access could benefit from advertising,
brochures, and social media. This provides a path to market to your current
base, but what about marketing to those in need that currently do not use the
library? Here are a few ideas.

> To reach those who are not engaged in the library, the best marketing
> approach applies the 80/20 rule, where you get 80 percent of the
> customers with 20 percent of the effort. Look for those opportunities
> where small efforts create the most impact. Set up a temporary
> library and exhibit at the city job fair to seek, engage, and educate
> both job seekers and the job givers. Set up a temporary library and
> exhibit at the state fair. Create a library night at the ballpark. Partner
> with charitable fundraising groups and their events. These are ideas

to get the ideas flowing. The point is to get the word out and use the 80/20 rule to change the conversation. You may or may not increase the number of cardholders through your effort, but you have exposed many people to your brand message, changed the conversation, and you have reached out to those who may need assistance.

Libraries should not be shy in using traditional media to get out their message. I have observed some of my library clients using their delivery trucks and bookmobiles to advertise. Some use billboard advertising as a very effective tool, and some even acquire PSA time from their local TV stations. Once again there is a lot of competition for your community's eyes and ears. As such to cut through the noise your advertisements must embrace a common brand message, which must be about more than just books. Imagine a national spot where a series of well-known celebrities say my favorite branding message in a quiet voice: "Sshhhh, can you hear the library working?" I am sure there are a number of celebrities (including famous writers) who would be more than happy to volunteer their time for a national media campaign. (However, once again, it must be more than just about books.)

Partnerships should be formed to support your campaign. Your local school libraries are a critical link in repairing the literacy steps of your community pyramid. Partner with your local school and host a library-sponsored storytime during back-to-school night. (The parents needing babysitters would be very grateful.) Invite school librarians to host a Q&A on the state of children's literacy at the public library. During National Library Card Signup Month, ask fast-food restaurants or coffee shops to give discounts on healthy food or drinks for anyone showing them a library book. Partnerships not only leverage your limited resources, but they also carry your brand message outside the walls of your library and then spread it throughout the community. This concept works with social media too. Steve relayed to me that when MCPL recently was awarded the IMLS National Medal, many of the library's partners, like school districts and chambers of commerce, for instance, cross-posted the announcement on their websites, Facebook profiles, and Twitter feeds.

Your library already markets your services to those outside your user base. Take a new look at your approach from the prism of the purpose-based library and your pyramid.

STEP 6
ESTABLISH A MARKETING BUDGET

I mentioned one of my lean mantras is "If you do not measure it, it must not be important." We can create a corollary statement to this truism: "If you do not fund it, it will not happen." Once your targeted marketing campaign including staffing and training requirements is established, the funding requirements should be apparent, and you will need seed money. I have presented the concepts of this book to corporations, foundations, and charities. The response has always been electric. I believe if your director presents the vision for your purpose-based library to select organizations, you will find your seed money. Furthermore, once your dashboard metrics are in place and your group can market the value-added impact the libraries have on the community, additional funding will flow to bolster your most effective programs. I believe the secret with these groups is establishing ownership in the concept. While you provide the vision, do not sell them on the idea, as the idea sells itself. Ask their advice and request guidance. Ask them to share their own story about community issues or challenges find out what their priorities are. Look for common ground and build upon it. If they want to take the lead, thank them and offer resources to assist.

STEP 7
CHANGE THE CONVERSATION
WITH VALUE-BASED DASHBOARD METRICS

The ultimate objective for libraries is to change the conversation from "Do we need libraries?" and "They just lend books," to "Libraries are at the center of our community transformation." We have our brand message and we have our advertisements, but an effective marketing campaign is not a one-way conversation. It must be a two-way conversation, then a three-way, and finally a conversation to influence the future funding of your library. You have recruited your fanatic and frequent users; now you must recruit the influential members of your community, those who influence the decision makers or are the decision makers themselves. Once again the key tool is establishing ownership in the idea, in this case, the library. Get them inside your doors by inviting them to speak to your Gold and Silver and Signature club members. Ask them for advice on how to get your message out. Seek them out when you find an obstacle in your way. Create social media groups based on each step of the pyramid. Create a new kind of book club but one based on the steps of the pyramid. Feed these groups with resource information. Once again imagine what a Friends of Child Literacy group and a Friends of Adult Literacy group could accomplish. Feed them your dashboard metrics. Get them engaged. Embrace your role as a community steward and facilitator. Change the conversation.

STEP 8
CREATE PORTALS OF EDUCATION, COMMUNICATION, AND CONNECTION

Ultimately your agent-of-change voices must translate into effective, actionable groups. Libraries as their facilitator must create portals so they can communicate and connect. People need to gather, to plan, to lead, and to act. The voices you recruit will be your first line of recruits to organize and act. Educate them on the pyramid and educate them on where the gaps lie. Solicit their ideas to improve, their ideas to organize, and their ideas to recruit others. Their actions and results will be your best marketing campaign. Libraries are not the force that will transform their communities; they are the means, the spark. You now have the flint, so start sparking.

Prominently display the pyramid on your website. For each step in the pyramid create a link that presents a portal into that particular dashboard metric's world. For example, imagine you click on the Functional Literacy and Access step of your pyramid on your library website. You are taken to a page where the literacy dashboard metrics are presented. Highlighted on the page are the dashboard metrics for high-risk third graders who do not like to read. The dashboard metric shows how much progress has been made over the years, and it ties it directly to the number of library storytimes conducted for at-risk children. On the page you see librarian-recommended books and articles on how to improve literacy in your community. You also see literacy links to TED Talks and local inspirational stories. You notice a link where you see opportunities to help, to volunteer, and a link indicating where funds are needed. You see a cart where you can donate funds. This is presented for every step in your pyramid. Check www.purposebasedlibrary.com for progress on purpose-based library software.

Sponsor business luncheons at the library where your business partners brainstorm on how to put ideas into action. Form separate business teams to focus on different steps of the pyramid. Use their resources, skills, experience, and funds to make a difference.

Create a Community Transformation Center in your library where the pyramid and the dashboard metrics are prominently displayed. Make the room prominent and visible; the first thing patrons see when they enter the library. Surround the area with books, media, and research tools to encourage people to engage. Create a brainstorming room for planned and unplanned meetings. Include a volunteer signup area managed by volunteers. Recruit your influential voices to speak not only at these events but to hang out in these transformation centers to recruit more voices. As previously stated, libraries have experience forming Friends of Library groups. Use that example to form many other groups focused on each step of the pyramid. Form and organize social media groups, use these groups to drive idea generation, transformation projects, and volunteer opportunities. Post your pyramid results on your website and your Facebook page. Create a social media engagement center in your library to encourage these online community members to interact face-to-face and keep in touch through social media.

STEP 9
CELEBRATE

Positivity sells. By highlighting the failures in your community, the community pyramid itself can easily take this marketing effort in a negative direction. Combat this negativity by constantly celebrating community achievements, no matter how small. Hold quarterly events to celebrate progress, send out quarterly updates in the form of newsletters, patron e-mails, and newspaper articles to tell your success stories. Dress up your library in a party atmosphere once a quarter to draw attention to the community's progress. Use Twitter, Facebook, and other social media venues to advertise and recruit members of the community to join in on these celebrations.

STEP 10
CREATE A 100-YEAR TRUTH AND VALUES PLAN

Japanese businesses are well-known for developing 500-year business plans. Their objective is to identify those truths and values that will assure their success beyond the present. Five hundred years seems a bit excessive, but the intent is to make sure today's issues and politics don't cloud long-term vision and to stay grounded in those unarguable truths and values of success and sustainability. It is sound policy, as too many businesses injure their long-term success for short-term gain. I believe the intent of a 500-year plan is to force members of the business to put aside their immediate and at times parochial views and look to what will ultimately be most beneficial to their business, their employees, and their community. The Japanese call this "truth and values." We believe libraries can benefit from a similar approach we call the "100-Year Truth and Values Plan."

We mentioned throughout the book the need for libraries to be stewards for their community. It is important to note that we did not use the term *advocate*. Libraries are one of the most trusted organizations in the United States; we believe it is mainly because they do not engage in political wars unless it relates to freedom of information and access for all. For our purpose-based library, this apolitical approach must remain. The role of the purpose-based librarian is to collect and present the dashboard metrics to lead the community to action but not play a role in interpreting, judging, or advocating a particular path or policy. That should be left to the community. The library should be an apolitical steward for their community pyramid, not a political advocate. The political wars of our time could easily be pulled into the pyramid; however, we have been very careful to define the pyramid in terms that everyone in the community can support. In other words, we seek a 100-year viewpoint and search for the truths and values from that perspective. The following provides our thoughts on the truths and values for our 100-year plan for your community.

Community Pyramid—100-Year Plan

15 Affirmations of Libraries' Common Truths and Values

1. If a person lacks food or shelter, we will ask how we can help and connect you to community members who can.
2. If people feel our community is unsafe or unsecure, we will provide the information and the resources to help empower our community to respond.
3. If a person seeks to improve his or her health, we will provide motivation, guidance, and information.
4. If a child struggles to read or use technology, we will offer resources and assistance.
5. If an adult struggles to function in society due to a lack of reading or technology skills, we will provide the tools and resources to help.
6. If a family has no access to books and information, we will provide them access.
7. If a child has no access to technology at home, we will provide access in other ways.
8. If a person has no access to their social community we will provide access.

9. If a person seeks assistance to improve basic job skills, we will provide resources and assistance.

10. If a person seeks employment, we will provide job search tools, guidance, and access to the community.

11. If a person seeks to connect to the community through volunteering, we will help make that connection.

12. If a person seeks to be entrepreneurial, we will provide communication resources, business information, guidance, and a desk.

13. If a person seeks to express a creative need, we will provide creative resources as well as an audience.

14. If a business seeks to improve our community, we will connect it.

15. If a person wishes to invest in our community, we will provide priorities, guidance, and the opportunity.

There is nothing political about this 100-year affirmation of truths and values. It is what is required to create, build, and maintain a healthy community. It is just good business. This should not be totally foreign to public libraries. It is not what Steve calls "purpose creep." Many of the values found in the 100-year plan can also be found in the public library service responses. I may be naïve, but I find it difficult to imagine anyone, regardless of political view, would argue with any of these truths and values. By presenting these 15 Affirmations of Libraries' Common Truths and Values, libraries can maintain their neutrality. We would propose that all libraries and their associations adopt these affirmations and present them to your community. We recommend that this 100-year plan be used to unite your efforts. We recommend you have your Signature club members sign the 100 Year Truth and Values Plan at a special signing ceremony. Hang the signed document prominently on your library walls. Whenever politics get in the way, pull out the 100-year plan and have everyone read the signatures. It will keep your groups focused on what is important and not allow the group to get caught up in the day-to-day issues we all are drawn to.

POTTER'S PERSPECTIVE, POINTS, AND PONDERINGS

Librarians and their staff are first to admit that they can improve their marketing efforts. There are reasons why libraries have difficulty marketing effectively.

First, many librarians say that they are marketing, but what they are really talking about is visual display merchandising. Displays are great and can be effective. But that's only one tool.

Second, when many librarians say they are marketing, they only focus on promotion. But there is more to marketing than just promotion; there is also price, product, and place (the four Ps of marketing). Promotion is fun and when done well it looks easy. But it isn't easy and requires an encompassing strategic approach to be effective. You cannot build a house only with a hammer. You need a vision, a plan, a foundation, the funding, the resources, and yes, nails. The same applies to marketing. An effective marketing effort requires a targeted plan, a strategy, and expected outcomes.

Third and most important, many librarians like to say that they are marketing, but they tend to not want to define target markets. More to the point, many bristle at exclusion, which is marketing to some, not to all. Libraries (especially public libraries) are egalitarian. It rubs many librarians wrong that we would promote here and not there. Isn't that unfair and unequal to the people that are "not there"? Consequently, we seek out those marketing approaches that target everyone. For example, my colleagues at MCPL used to love to "paper the town" in bookmarks. We didn't tailor messages. But marketing by definition is tailoring messages and excluding people outside the target market. Trying to market to all and not to a few creates an uphill struggle to be effective. Let me share a case study from my library.

Targeted Marketing Case Study

During our summer reading effectiveness study, we discovered in the pilot that our efforts with at-risk kids were paying very high dividends. To build upon this success, our youth services manager created a targeted marketing campaign to encourage our Title I schools to fully participate. Frankly, these Title I kids were starting a mile behind the starting line. The chances of them hitting grade-level reading by third grade were slight. But if we engaged them, we knew we could make a difference.

When we told our staff about the strategy, there was some pushback. Was it "fair" not to promote our program in school X, Y, and Z? Those kids need us too. Of course, the parents of those kids are breaking down the library door every week during the summer to assure those kids are participating. Those kids are reading above grade level. Do they need our program? Sure. Do they need to be encouraged to participate? Nope . . . Mom's got it covered. So a soft sell in these schools should be fine, and a full court press in Title I schools is warranted.

It really is important to target your markets and your messages. Every time you create a new brochure or bookmark or any piece of communication to your customers, first ask, "Who is the audience?" If your answer is "everyone," then try to concentrate on a primary customer to receive the message. When you can picture the profile of who is to receive the message, you will notice that the message becomes more personal. The appeal becomes more pointed and specific. The benefit becomes much more significant. When you tailor your message to specific markets, your message is much more effective. Will this mean that you might have to make three different messages on the bookmarks for your new program? Yes. It could mean that because you are trying to appeal to three different markets with one program. Always remember one of my favorite heuristics: "Market to everyone and you market to no one."

I would like to give a little advice about social media. Like so many efforts around marketing and promotion, social media looks much different than what it really is. At MCPL, we have one person solely dedicated to managing our social media presence (Facebook, Twitter, Pinterest, and Instagram). He is very talented and creative. While these services are great for getting your message out, they can also be dangerous. What if someone starts posting false things about the library? What if someone posts an inappropriate picture on your Instagram or Facebook wall? It is important to consider these possibilities and how you will address them when they inevitably do occur. Also, like your library collection (or a good garden) you have to work on your social media presence. Create, cultivate, manage, and maintain your presence. You have to constantly add new content and interact with your virtual customers, just like you do with your physical customers. You also need to consider purchasing post promotion. This will allow your stories to show up more broadly but also more targeted to your community. Our Facebook posts routinely have 75 to 80 percent better reach than the average post. You can find this kind of data on the Insights tab. For instance, I know that the last time we asked, "What are you reading?" more than 2,300 people saw the post organically without any special promotion or the purchase of ads. When you visit your page, you see how many Likes you have and how many people have posted. But by drilling into the "insight," you can tell how many messages are reaching your community.

NOTES

1. "2012 ZIP Code Business Patterns (NAICS)," US Census Bureau, May 2014, http://censtats.census.gov/cgi-bin/zbpnaic/zbpsect.pl.

2. "Whispers," *Austin Monitor*, July 28, 2014, www.infactdaily.com/newsread.cfm.

19
Philanthropy

IN THIS CHAPTER WE DISCUSS HOW THE PURPOSE-BASED library is better positioned to market value-added propositions to their community and their philanthropic supporters than simple book circulation numbers.

In the previous chapter we presented a framework for an effective marketing strategy, a way to change the conversation. Our ultimate goal is for libraries to not only survive, but to succeed and ultimately grow their services to the community. Growth of new services requires new funding, and therefore philanthropic community members (both large and small) are your key to move beyond success to growth at this top step of the pyramid.

Libraries would not exist or have survived if it were not for the likes of Benjamin Franklin and Andrew Carnegie. They may not have survived the transition to computers without the help of Bill Gates. Your new library would not have been built if not for the philanthropic generosity of your community members. Library directors will tell you their toughest job, especially in these current economic conditions, is to raise funds to build new branches. Make no mistake—the philanthropic members of your community are asking the same question as many others: "Are libraries still relevant?"

Having the purpose-based library and their metrics is like having a bullhorn in your hand. Yes, libraries are relevant, and here is why. These dashboard metrics provide the library director effective tools to draw attention to specific cracks in the community pyramid as well as specific actions that will help fill those gaps. It may not be building a new branch, but it might be funding an intern program, a neighborhood watch, outreach storytime events, and so on. These specific metrics will make a big difference in funding success. Furthermore, as libraries become the focal point for local businesses, charities, and neighborhoods, their value to the community will be better understood and the supporting library funds and endowments will follow.

I was asked how I might use the dashboard metrics to solicit a philanthropic member of the community to invest in this concept. Here would be my approach:

1. I would use this book to prepare to discuss the concepts of the pyramid. Prepare a presentation and arrange a meeting with my target audience.

2. When setting up the meeting, I would emphasize that I am not looking for money, but I am looking for advice.

3. If possible, I would arrange the meeting at the library, but I would not push it. If my target audience wants me to come to them, by all means I would do so. If they do come to the library, I would make sure the library has a storytime and other programs going on in the background. I would work with the library to assure all the computers were full and that there was a waiting line.

4. I would present the concepts of the pyramid and the plan to create dashboard metrics for each. I would emphasize that this is a value-based concept and understanding cause-and-effect relationships is our objective. I would show them an example dashboard developed for our community.

5. I would ask them to share their own stories about their community experience and where they think the library should focus attention. If they express no preference, I would be prepared to present library stories from the various steps in the pyramid where people's lives have changed. But I would emphasize that what we are doing is not enough as evidenced by the dashboard metrics.

6. I would provide examples on how I plan to value the programs we are pursuing to effect these priority metrics.

7. I would ask them advice on how the library could best effect change in the community, and I would be prepared to state that the library is stepping up to be the focal point for the effort.

8. I would finish with my strongest point. I would provide a vision of a future where each community and library across the country are an incubator for programs and ideas. I would propose that the library would be the facilitator of collecting, organizing, and sharing the best of these programs based on value-added metrics. I would ask them to imagine a future where the transformation comes not from the top, but primarily from the communities themselves.

9. I would thank them for their time.

10. Once complete I would work with the library and their research/reference librarians to further collect data on the pyramid steps my target audience is most interested in.

11. I would work with the library staff to evaluate existing programs and brainstorm new ideas and programs to impact these targeted steps that are in scope of the library's strategic direction.

12. I would bring in my business partners and have them brainstorm with me on what programs they think would be most effective.

13. I would create a pilot program and solicit these businesses to help guide the program and to assure the metrics are properly defined and measured.

14. Once the pilot is complete, and I have tangible results and metrics, I would request a follow-up meeting with my targeted philanthropic audience and present my results.

15. I would request their feedback, ideas, and money to expand the duration and scope of the program.

16. I would send them quarterly progress reports on the results of the program, specifically the dashboard metrics, to show them the value of their investment—even if they did not donate any funds.

While this example focused on a foundation or business, the same approach would apply to an individual. For many of you, individual giving may outpace corporate and foundation giving. What is important is that you know your audience and you tailor your message to that audience. Sandra Swanson, president of OrangeBoy, provided the following advice:

> Giving, like marketing, is about the individual and how they see themselves playing a role in the organization. It's up to the organization to do their homework about the donor, whether it's an individual, foundation or corporation and find a way for that donor to participate.

We recommend the philanthropic dashboard metrics shown in figure 19.1.

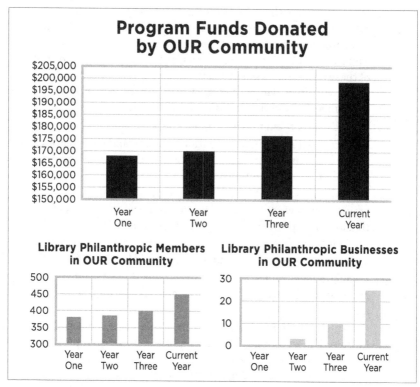

FIGURE 19.1
Program development

POTTER'S PERSPECTIVE, POINTS, AND PONDERINGS

There are interesting challenges while fund-raising for a library. One major challenge is the question of relevance. Given our recent economic conditions, it is difficult for a local community foundation to choose to help a library over a homeless shelter or a skills-training program. To a degree, those funders are correct; they are trying to make a difference at the base of our pyramid. But we haven't been helping ourselves. Focusing on quantitative outputs rather than qualitative outcomes will always make libraries look less relevant. Making the shift to outcomes helps with fund-raising.

Perhaps you are forward thinking and you have developed a great program that is outcome based, only to be charged with mission creep. These issues come up when funders see your request as something outside what you should be doing. A librarian once told me about a library in the late 1960s and early 1970s that had their own bus service and youth basketball leagues. These are pretty obvious examples of mission creep. This happens when an organization chases the money and starts to lose sight of the mission. Be careful not to chase the money. When you do, often you find yourself spread even thinner and spending a lot of time doing things that do not help you fulfill your purpose. Thus each library must look to their pyramid's value-based metrics and match their efforts with the most important needs of their community, including existing efforts.

There have been a few libraries that have been successful in attracting people to fund successful existing programs. For instance, if your summer reading program is wildly successful why not approach the funding community to help you sustain the program? Pitch the program as if it were a fairly new program. Sadly, you'll find that several people of affluence and influence in your community don't even know about your 40-year SRP. That may be sad, but use it to your advantage. Show the funders your good output data, but stress your more impressive outcome data. You will find that people will be willing to help you fund this program. But why go after money for something that you are already doing and that you are already funding? First, people like to back a winner. Showing that you have a good, fundable idea is one thing. Showing that you are positioned to implement your good idea puts you in a better position. Showing that you can prove success is a great position to be in. Second, allowing people to link to programs that appeal to their conscience and heart allows you to make a greater impact and stronger engagement. Finally, freeing up regular revenue from a successful program can allow using that money and those resources to try new programs. Frankly, it may be easier to get someone to fund your old tried-and-tested idea, especially when backed by concrete metrics and results, than to take a flier on an unproven and untried concept. The good news is that many of the ideas and concepts presented in this book are already programs that libraries support; however, as this book proposes, many elements are missing: community engagement, partnerships, and most important, value-added metrics. Add these concepts to existing programs and you can sell anew.

20
Library Presentation

IN THE PREVIOUS CHAPTER WE PRESENTED A MARKETING PLAN to change the conversation about libraries. In this chapter we extend this marketing plan by proposing that the physical presentation of your library should be aligned with your marketing effort and your community pyramid. We envision a means for the purpose-based library to reintroduce themselves to the community by changing how they present themselves. Specifically, we suggest the physical presentation of your library should reflect the purpose-based library and the value-added services they provide.

I have worked at and toured countless libraries. Typically you enter through the security gates and you see the new book area, the circulation desk, and then the various stacks organized by nonfiction, fiction, and so on. This is the standard layout most libraries follow. Lately there has been a movement to further reorganize libraries to look more like a Barnes & Noble bookstore. In fact I have helped on projects to do just that. I have changed my mind. If the library is designed to reflect a retail distribution center, this is exactly how your patrons will see you and place value upon you. The purpose-based library should not reflect a bookstore; it should reflect your purpose to seek, engage, and transform. It should reflect the community pyramid you are dedicated to build and repair.

We propose a new concept for the purpose-based library. As we suggested in chapter 18, step 8, as you enter through the front doors the first thing that draws your eye is the Community Transformation Center. There, prominently presented, you see the dashboard metrics, a community improvement calendar of events, a place to volunteer your time, and a volunteer at the desk to answer your questions. Around the Community Transformation Center you find books and media prominently displayed on the topics of community improvement and volunteerism. Next you see the children's area, but it is now called the Children's Literary Center. In the Children's Literacy Center you see PCs dedicated to literacy improvement as well as software games and fun educational programs. Surrounding the area are children's books and the storytime area. Prominently displayed are the children's literacy dashboard metrics. Past the Children's Literacy Center you notice a number of creative labs, one for music, one for arts, and one for the maker lab. Topical books, music sheets, or art supplies surround each area. In the back you see the Adult Literacy Center, where PCs are dedicated to self-driven literacy software as well as books geared to adult literacy. The adult literacy dashboard is displayed. You then notice the incubator lab, where numerous worktables are arranged and retired business volunteers lead a discussion with a number of start-up entrepreneurs. This area is supported with dedicated computers, printers, and phones for the group and is surrounded by government business forms and business books. Near this area is the internship program where interns are building their foundational skills. A list of business sponsors is prominently advertised. You then see the Entertainment Center of the library, where numerous patrons are engaged in social networking on public computers. Surrounding this area are books of fiction as well as entertainment media. In another section you see the Knowledge Center, where posters advertise upcoming webinars, TED Talks, and planned speaker events. Surrounding this area are the nonfiction books and nonfiction media.

As we discussed in chapter 17, library staff spend a great deal of time managing customer accounts, assisting checkouts, and scheduling and managing the public PC area. More often than not they are stationed behind a desk. A large percentage of the purpose-based library staff and technicians must become mobile, seeking and engaging patrons in the various centers. The smaller libraries could follow this same concept but of course be presented in a more consolidated space. However the point is that the areas would be delineated and advertised based on the value you provide to your community and how you want your community to see you. The presentation of your layout becomes your best marketing tool. Is your library just a book distribution center, or it is a library that is so much more? The purpose-based library's layout and presentation would make it clear to your patrons your community mission, your purpose, and how valuable you are to the community's health and well-being.

POTTER'S PERSPECTIVE, POINTS, AND PONDERINGS—AND PET PEEVES

The Barnes & Noble model requires me to respond, as it is one of my pet peeves. The whole "Barnes & Nobling" of the public library missed the mark. What appeals to people at B&N is that it is comfortable and rational. Before the B&N stores showed up, libraries put four hard wooden chairs at 3 x 5 foot tables and called that the reading area. The expectation was that people would sit, four to a table, and not sit for more than an hour (because the chairs wouldn't allow it!). The lighting was harsh and headache inducing. The books had to be shelved spine-out for maximum space efficiency, to make it easy to reshelve, and for the staff to easily find things. The customer (and the community) was a secondary thought.

So, B&N helped us rethink how to be hospitable. But we missed the point. All our decisions should be driven by strategic alignment of the library's purpose, not a bookstore's purpose. Coffee shops, maker spaces, print-on-demand book machines, and 3-D printers are all very cool, but if they are not aligned with the library's purpose, we are missing the mark. The purpose-based library should be strategically aligned with how best to serve the community. The community pyramid guides the way and the metrics establish our priorities. Our library's buildings, resources, and staff should reflect this strategic alignment.

21

Closing the Gap with Your
Suppliers and Customers

IN THIS CHAPTER WE EXAMINE THE CONCEPTS OF "PULL"
versus "push" demand management systems. We propose that pull systems
get you closer to both your customer and your suppliers. We also propose that
by embracing a pull system while leveraging libraries' cross-country footprint
you can gather a stronger voice, lower costs, and expand your services, all leading to growth.

The concepts of lean began our discussion on survival. Lean will also end
our discussion on growth. As we have established, the Toyota Production System (TPS) developed in the late 1970s was the precursor to lean. One of the
fundamental philosophies of TPS is the concept of pull versus push demand
management. Pull states that you should allow the customer to pull demand
from an organization rather than the organization pushing demand onto the
customer. While simple in concept, it is powerful in practice. The Japanese and
now most American manufacturers call this the Kanban system. For a simple
example, let us imagine a future where you bought two bottles of ketchup at
the grocery store. When you place a bottle of ketchup in your refrigerator, the
refrigerator recognizes the bottle and reads the item into its inventory. You
place the second bottle in the pantry. A few weeks later the ketchup bottle
in the refrigerator is empty, so you remove it and then place the second bottle from the pantry into the refrigerator, where it reads this new bottle into

inventory. The refrigerator sends a note to your smartphone grocery list to buy another bottle of ketchup. Now when you pull a bottle off the shelf at the grocery store and buy it, the grocery store's inventory system signals to the store buyer that another bottle of ketchup was sold. When enough ketchup bottles have been sold that match the lead-time of delivery, the system signals to the ketchup supplier to send more ketchup bottles just in time to the store and just before they run out of bottles on the shelf. The same system is set up for the ketchup suppliers to the bottler, who also have their own pull Kanban system, triggering the resupply of tomatoes, empty ketchup bottles, sugar, vinegar, and so on. By pulling that ketchup bottle off the shelf from the grocer, you and others have rippled through the system and eventually signaled to the suppliers to react from these pulls. Nothing is produced in the service chain unless a signal from the prior link asks for more. This eliminates waste throughout the system.

The opposite of the pull system is the push system. In this environment, a forecaster is assigned the job of guessing how much demand the store will have for bottled ketchup. Assume last year was a long, hot summer and as a result it was a big year for ketchup, and the buyer assumes the same will happen this year. In fact he is an optimist and expects even more growth. He makes his best guess and orders boxes of bottled ketchup to be delivered to the grocery store. This forecast ripples through the system and all the vendors plan their manufacturing on these and their own optimistic forecasts. However, it turns out that the main salsa vendor for grocery stores in the southwest launched a big marketing campaign with large discounts. Salsa sales surge, and bottled ketchup sales plummet. To make room for the salsa in the warehouse and their shelves, the grocery stores stop orders of bottled ketchup to the vendor. The ketchup bottle manufacturer had already built a large inventory of stock in anticipation of large sales. They shut down production. This ripples down to all the suppliers and eventually leads to rotten tomatoes on someone's shipping dock. The push system guesses what the customer needs and wants, and the forecaster crosses his fingers that he is right. The pull system does not guess; it only responds to what the customer really wants.

The key to all of this is lead time. The longer the lead time between the supplier of tomatoes to the ketchup manufacturing plant, the more guessing you have to do and the more inaccurate it becomes. With long lead times, you order a lot, requiring large commitments of cash, larger warehouses, and more people to move the material around. With shorter lead times, suppliers can respond more quickly to the changing demand and deliver what is needed just in time. This requires much less investment in cash, smaller warehouses, and fewer forklifts.

For the book publishing industry, the same push versus pull model exists. An author writes a book and the publisher forecasts how many print books it needs to manufacture and hopes it was correct. Amazon's entry into the publishing world is a perfect case study. From the *Wall Street Journal*:

> Amazon.com Inc. has had lots of success in book retailing. But cracking the publishing business hasn't been as easy. Take one of Amazon's biggest titles for fall, actress and director Penny Marshall's memoir "My Mother Was Nuts." In its first four weeks on sale, it has sold just 7,000 copies in hardcover, according to Nielsen BookScan. By comparison, actor Rob Lowe's memoir, 2011's "Stories I Only Tell My Friends," published by Macmillan's Henry Holt & Co., sold 54,000 hardcover copies in its first four weeks.[1]

This is a perfect example of how a negative message does not sell and positive one does. Forbes.com also weighed in,

> $47: The amount Amazon Publishing paid "Laverne & Shirley" star Penny Marshall for every print copy it sold of her memoir, "My Mother Was Nuts." Marshall received an $800,000 advance, but the title only sold 17,000 copies.[2]

This is push forecasting at its worst. Libraries, in anticipation of large sales, may have fallen into the same trap and bought or leased a large number of copies of Penny Marshall's book as well. How many books did Amazon print to support their $800,000 advance? Who knows? But my guess is quite a lot. This is all because of the long lead time to publish the print version of the book.

In the first part of this book, on survival, we emphasize the need to embrace lean, not for the reduction in costs but because of the improvement in customer service. This improvement comes from eliminating all the waste in a process and thus shrinking the delivery lead time of a service. The leaner you get, the shorter the lead time required to deliver the product, and therefore the closer and closer you get to your customer's true expression of demand. The leaner you get, the less forecasting and demand guessing required. Ultimately, you shrink lead times to the point at which you can successfully allow the customers to pull demand from you and only produce another product when they actually ask for it.

Therefore, the ultimate expression of lean is e-books. The lead-time to delivery of an e-book is miniscule, seconds. Yes, there is cataloging and linking to do, but even that can be streamlined to minutes. Allowing the customer to pull demand rather than pushing one's guesses onto the customer is a game changer. Less investment in books, less physical space needed to store books, less staff to receive, move, process, move, discharge, move, deliver, receive, move, print, move, and stock those books. A large library that just delivers e-books would need only a handful of staff. However, this smaller staff is not a path to success and growth. It is a path to obsolescence. The purpose-based library would seek to shift more and more of their collection to e-books to embrace the concept of pull demand. The purpose-based library would promote and train their customers to love e-books. The purpose-based library would free up staff from moving books around to seek, engage, and transform their community.

Pull demand management in combination with e-books as well as the potential to leverage the footprint of libraries presents an even more exciting possibility. I like to write a book each Christmas for my young nieces and nephews (and hopefully not too long from now, my grandchildren). Based on feedback from my client children's librarians, my last effort is good enough to be published. However, to get a publisher's attention, you need an agent. As a writer without an agent, you truly feel like a man on an island waving to the ocean to get attention. I am a busy guy, and doing the work to find an honest and capable agent is just not on my priority list. However, a great book is just waiting to be published and enjoyed by thousands of children.

During my trip to Amelia Island I walked past a man sitting at a table near the front door of an independent bookstore. He had made himself available to sign his recently self-published children's book about pirates. I stopped and turned around, as I could not resist interviewing him. I learned that the bookstore owner sponsors local self-published authors by connecting them with an indie-publishing group and also dedicates a section of his bookstore to these local indie authors. I felt pain for this guy because he lived on a small island, not only geographically, but also from a marketing point of view. He will have great difficulty getting his book exposed to any market beyond this small island. If he is lucky he will sell a hundred or so copies. Nonetheless, I loved the partnership between the bookstore (a market outlet) and the self-published author.

However, what if the Fernandina Beach Public Library manager sent the Nassau County Library selector a recommendation to add this book to the collection? What if this Nassau County Library selector was a part of a larger group of selectors in Florida who shared their resources to review and select indie-published books? And what if these Florida selectors of indie-published books served as an incubator and they recommended the best "sellers" of this incubation to all the selectors in North America? If this were in place, the author of the pirate book may very well have his book in every library in the country—all started by a branch manager in Florida.

Indie and self-publishing are trends that are not going away, and with e-books they are becoming more and more attractive options for writers. The start-up cost is less for an e-book than for a hard copy, and it is much easier and less costly to distribute and update.

It is ironic that while e-books are actually less costly to produce and distribute, the costs of e-books have become a major issue for libraries. Every library knows that the publishers are anything but friendly partners in the library's attempt to increase their e-book collection.

To grow, libraries must change the game and bypass those who seek to control the publishing world, especially when it comes to e-books. By forming library selector consortiums organized within states that feed a larger audience of selectors nationwide, libraries can catch the indie wave by pulling local indie demand to become a leader and not a follower in the publishing game. As you expose and market these indie books to your customers, your customers can tell you what books they want. They will pull the demand from you, and you will pull the demand from these print-on-demand indie publishers. Considering the conflict between Amazon and indie publishers, libraries have an opportunity to become a major voice in the discussion.

The pull demand management model changed the game for lean manufacturers. They learned that it made sense to locate their suppliers as close to the end manufacturer as possible. Imagine the ketchup manufacturer with the bottle supplier next door to the plant and both plants surrounded by a tomato farmer. The entire service chain is streamlined, and they all can respond to the changing pulls from their customers. Imagine if libraries could actually pull their demand from an indie publisher that lived next door to the branch and would print on demand each time a customer requested that book. Crazy? It is happening already, and Steve is the one doing it.

Steve has created his own print-on-demand publishing house at his new Woodneath Library Center. Steve plans to offer resources allowing authors to self-publish, and he also plans to select the best of these to add to his collection. Steve has proven that libraries cannot only build relationships with local indie publishers, but they can also become indie publishers themselves. The following case study puts a fine point on the concept that libraries can become much more than just distributers of content—they can facilitate the creation of value content.

THE STORY CENTER AT WOODNEATH—CASE STUDY

The Story Center at Woodneath is a very different, but very holistic, way to view story creation in the 21st century. The concept starts with a focus on the story itself. Everyone has a story or group of things that expresses experience. Sometimes that story takes the form of a memoir. Sometimes that story takes the form of 20 poems. Sometimes that story is a collection of recipes that remind you of your childhood. These are all stories. But if you want to share these stories, you will have to tell them in a way that is engaging and relatable to an audience. At the Story Center, there will be single classes focused on a specific task. There will also be classes with multiple meetings to teach important concepts. Programmatic partners like members of the National Storytelling Network or the Writer's Place of Kansas City will frequently teach these classes. To further strengthen community, peer review panels will be created so authors can improve each other's work.

Once the story is improved and ready, then the important question of media is considered. Some stories are going to be printed books. Some stories will be e-books. Some stories will be audio recordings. Some stories might even be video vignettes. The Story Center will have the equipment available to capture the story in the right medium. Part of publishing the story will include a distribution right for the library and the right to distribute an e-book or eAudio version of the work. This will allow Mid-Continent Public Library to create a publishing imprint, assign ISBNs, create MARC records, and load that information to the OCLC database (for any items MCPL adds to the collection).

What does the library gain from this model?

- As mentioned previously, the library views the Story Center as a holistic approach to literacy.
- The library also helps to build a stronger community through the collection and distribution of the region's stories.
- The library also fosters the fledgling content creator's community.
- By setting up a way for self-published authors to improve their works, the library helps to improve the quality of the self-published content in the library's collection.
- The library develops a supply of quality content. All businesses long to have control over their supplies.
- The library develops relationships that create additional programming opportunities.
- The library creates a small revenue stream by distributing items created at the Story Center.

What does the author gain from this model?

- The author learns new skills that can be applied in all walks of life.
- The author meets a community of people interested in similar activities and topics.
- Self-published authors routinely miss out on editorial assistance from publishers. The Story Center provides a form of this through peer review.
- Self-published authors routinely miss out on distribution assistance from publishers. The Story Center will have the ability to distribute works.
- Self-published authors routinely miss out on publicity that publishers traditionally offer. The library system alone will

provide 31 locations for authors to "tour" and promote their works.

- Through partnerships, the Story Center will be able to sell, distribute, and circulate e-book versions of the work.
- The author gains access to special hardware and software that is cost prohibitive for many first timers.
- The author's work can be more widely discovered through the EspressNet print-on-demand network and through OCLC if MCPL adds the item to the library collection.

If we were talking about professional baseball, the Story Center at Woodneath would be something similar to the Arizona Instructional League, without the million-dollar signing bonuses! People with desire will come to learn more about this craft and to develop skills. Some will discover they don't have the chops. Some will learn some interesting skills to apply to other parts of their lives. Some will move up to the next level.

LIBRARY SELECTOR CONSORTIUMS

Libraries looking to secure their future should take a very close look at the Woodneath model.

Consider the following:

- Self-publishing is growing leaps and bounds.
- Marketing and distribution are the biggest obstacles for self-published authors.
- Libraries have a huge and instant market.
- A children's book in every library will market itself at no cost.
- E-books are the future.
- Publishers are trying to control the amount of e-books distributed by the library market.

All these issues point to an opportunity for libraries to partner with self-published, independent authors. However with the exception of few local authors, collection development groups have shied away from buying self-published authors' books for many good reasons, including:

- Sometimes the books have content that is not appropriate.
- The books have not been properly edited.
- The graphics do not meet professional publishing standards.
- There are too many of them to review for quality.
- The volumes are too small, eliminating economy of scale.

- The time it takes to find, sort through, evaluate, and select these items is prohibitive.
- Without a publisher overseeing the content, some items have copyright violations and other issues with intellectual property.

All of these concerns are valid. However, the Woodneath Story Center model shows us a way to overcome these obstacles and develop a statewide, even nationwide, publishing arm for public libraries.

We propose an online version of the Story Center. A library-based writer's curriculum would exist throughout the country and bring together authors, graphic artists, and editors to bring their book to a publishable state. The local selector would cull the offerings and select those they believe worthy of incubation. A group of selectors from across the state would be formed to review all of these offerings and select those they believe have value for statewide recommendation. Those selected would be presented on a common site for all library selectors across the country to review. By combining the resources of all the libraries across the nation, library-driven self-publishing could take over the self-publishing world. Libraries would market the books they select with reviews on their website to help expose their patrons to these self-published works. Oh, and of course the cost of the book to the library would be greatly discounted because of the marketing value that libraries add to the equation. If the book becomes popular enough, the author would have opportunities to negotiate with the larger publishing houses.

And finally, to follow our view that libraries should physically present themselves in terms of the purpose-based library, we envision a sign above one of your book stacks that says "Incubator Lab." In this incubator section of your library you would include all the books, CDs, and e-books from local indie writers who the library sponsored. By cleverly marketing this section you can encourage your patrons to be a part of the incubation process. Imagine the creative possibilities for this area!

We see this library/indie self-publishing concept as an opportunity to create a larger voice for libraries in the publishing arena, a voice that is currently not being heard. For example, I believe this is a way to leapfrog the obstacles that now exist with e-book publishers that are pricing libraries out of the market. I also believe this approach will bring them back to the negotiating table with a more reasonable pricing model.

POTTER'S PERSPECTIVE, POINTS, AND PONDERINGS

There hasn't been a more transformative and significant change in the library world than the introduction of digital content. But nothing really shook the foundation of librarianship like the recent adoption of e-books.

Interestingly, the Amazon Kindle was not the first try at e-books. In 1991, Sony introduced the Discman, which displayed the text of books from CD-ROM discs. It was heavy and clunky. Many people saw this as the first time a company tried to develop a dedicated device for reading. But this was very early in the story. Consider that in 1991 most of the world didn't know about the internet and the World Wide Web hadn't been invented yet. A successful adoption of the Discman would have assumed large consumer adoption with libraries buying "books" on CD-ROM or DVD to check out to people, still coming to the local library to pick up and return the physical media. There wasn't much available apart from reference titles for the Discman. The content, or lack of it, ultimately doomed the Discman.

In 1998, a company called NuvoMedia launched the Rocket eBook. This was very promising. It was about the size of a paperback but weighed about as much as a hardback. It had a backlit screen and could read books from small-press content providers like Peanut Press. Ultimately Barnes & Noble provided content for the Rocket eBook. At $500 a unit, most people wouldn't be purchasing these themselves, so a few libraries purchased them to demonstrate the service. Content was hard to obtain and difficult to load on the device. Additionally, users were limited to a monochrome screen and images were very limited. NuvoMedia was buoyed by the 1990s dot.com bubble. With the market correction, much of the anticipated growth did not occur. And the Rocket eBook had the same issue with content that the Discman had. People quickly discovered that the gadget was all right and something that people could grow accustomed to working. However, the lack of good content really held this device back too. Finally, RCA bought the Rocket eBook and eventually pulled the plug on the project a few years before the introduction of the Kindle and the Nook.

Before the Kindle, there was one more attempt to launch an e-book reader. The Sony Reader hit the market in 2006, a year before the Kindle. It was the first device to dip below $500. But, much like the Rocket eBook and the Discman, lack of content and the high price of the device slowed adoption.

Everything changed in 2007 when Amazon launched the Kindle. Why was it different this time? Simply because Amazon had something that Sony, RCA, and NuvoMedia didn't have. Amazon had leverage to "encourage" the publishing houses to create digital versions of the content that people wanted to read. Two years later, Barnes & Noble used a similar strategy to open up content from their traditional publishing partners. If there is one lesson that can be drawn from the various false starts around the adoption of the e-book, it is that content matters. Content really, really matters. Without access to high-quality content that readers want, e-book readers won't be adopted and demand for the devices will dry up.

It is safe to say that there has been an adoption of e-books and e-book readers. The Kindle and iPad are not headed the way of the Rocket eBook any time soon. So now the question becomes how do libraries work within this new environment?

There have been several interesting developments around e-content acquisition and distribution in the library world over the past several years. But before getting into those developments, it is important to understand something fundamental about e-books: they are not books. This may seem obvious, but it is not. E-book content is actually considered a computer file. The e-book on your iPhone or Kindle is a series of ones and zeros, or bits and bytes. This computer code can be an analog to a print-on-paper book, but it isn't the same thing. Consequently, a computer file is governed by the end-user license agreement. This means that concepts from copyright, like the first-sale doctrine for instance, don't apply to e-books or really any computer file of any kind. In general terms, nearly all computer licenses give the purchasers the right to use it but ownership of the file remains with the license holder (not necessarily the purchaser).

Understanding that an e-book and a book are two very different things that are even governed by different laws and regulations is very important. It isn't clear that this distinction was apparent to publishers and e-book vendors just a few years ago. Clearly, the dispute that the Kansas State Library had with OverDrive underscores this point. As you likely recall, the Kansas State Library contested ownership of the e-content provided by their contractor, OverDrive. Although the library secured access to the desired content, by 2010 end-user license agreements had been clarified so it was clear that a library did not actually own the license they acquired for their customers. Additionally, the unilateral restrictions that publishers place on their e-content (e.g., Harper Collins and the requirement to relicense titles after 26 circulations) create unique stress between libraries, publishers, and vendor partners.

During this upheaval, Jamie LaRue at the Douglas County (CO) Library developed an interesting solution. What if a library became "OverDrive?" LaRue set up an Adobe Content Server, made arrangements with the Colorado Independent Publishers Association, and changed the formula. With the library in a more critical position, it could deal with a publisher and set up much more favorable conditions.

The "Douglas County Model" is not without its critics. Some have suggested that there isn't much "selection" occurring when libraries apply this model. While there is nothing wrong with becoming a repository for everything published by a given association, there is a lot of chaff that comes with that wheat. Additionally, many libraries that have tried to replicate the model have found it very difficult to get the technology to work. This doesn't mean that libraries should not try to acquire their own content. Developing independent content seems to be a very natural thing for a library to do in the 21st century. However, libraries have to be careful not to abdicate their selection duties. Just because a library can add every title doesn't mean that it should. People expect libraries to have considered the quality of the items in their collection. Does the book meet the library's collection development strategy? If it does, it should be added. If it doesn't, even if it has nominal costs, it shouldn't be added.

When new media comes to the scene or new technology arrives that is cost prohibitive, libraries frequently form consortia. In Missouri, there have been cataloging consortia, a 16 mm film co-op, and consortia online database purchasing through the Missouri Research and Education Network (MOREnet). Given the history of sharing, it really wasn't surprising to find Missouri librarians banding together to form MO-Libraries-To-Go. This is a consortium of medium-sized public libraries, administered through the Missouri Library Network Corporation (now Amigos Library Services) that share access to a single collection of OverDrive e-content. These libraries would not be able to join OverDrive independently. However, joined together, they share content, expenses, training, and administrative costs.

Libraries have always been about collecting stories and sharing those stories with the community. Traditionally, that has meant buying a book that has been through an editorial process and through the library's collection development process. Then that book is loaned to the community. Digital content is really just the latest development in this same old story. While it is challenging and making libraries think in new ways, in several ways it is what libraries have always done.

NOTES

1. Jeffrey A. Trachtenberg, "Amazon Struggles to Crack Publishing," *Wall Street Journal*, last updated October 17, 2012, http://online.wsj.com/news/articles/ SB10000872396390444592704578062631678116120.

2. Jeff Bercovici, "Amazon vs. Book Publishers, By the Numbers," *Forbes.com*, Tech, February 10, 2014, www.forbes.com/sites/jeffbercovici/2014/02/10/ amazon-vs-book-publishers-by-the-numbers.

PART IV

Sustainability

Ken Burns, known best for his series on the Civil War, produced a new series for PBS called *The Dust Bowl*. Being from Oklahoma, it piqued my interest. The series was both fascinating and frightening. Encouraged by the government, farmers plowed up millions of acres of grass and grazing land to plant wheat. Shortly thereafter a horrible drought plagued the land, creating what we now call the Dust Bowl. The soil, uncovered and no longer having its historical root system of grasses, blew violently throughout a 150,000-square-mile area. The most poignant moments of the series show cows found dead with their bellies full of dust and that many women committed suicide because they could not keep the dust not only out of their homes, but also their cupboards. By 1940 2.5 million people had fled this region of Oklahoma, Kansas, Texas, Colorado, and New Mexico.[1]

Guymon, Oklahoma, the epicenter of the Dust Bowl, is located nearly six hours by car from my hometown of Tulsa and is in many ways unfamiliar to most of us who live in Eastern Oklahoma. Tulsa is called Green Country, located at the foothills of the Ozark Mountains, while Guymon is located squarely in the flatlands of the Oklahoma Panhandle. However, I do have a connection to Guymon, as I remained friends with a girl from Guymon I met in college and who now lives in my neighborhood. Knowing that her family had lived in Guymon for quite a long time, I asked her if she had any stories about the Dust Bowl. Her answer surprised me; she knew little of the Dust Bowl or its history.

Confucius is quoted as saying, "Study the past if you would define the future."[2] The following article excerpt from the *Washington Post* portends a vision of a returning dust bowl:

> The [Ogallala Aquifer] water feeds the nearly one-fifth of the wheat, corn, cattle and cotton grown in the United States. Researchers found that 30 percent of the Kansas portion of the Ogallala Aquifer has already been pumped out, and another 39 percent will get used up in the next half-century at existing rates. Kansas, clearly, is on the fast track to depletion. As a result, agriculture production is likely to peak around 2040 and decline after that.[3]

The authors of this article are not optimistic and predict that the southwest and northwest will soon follow the fate of the west central district in terms of water shortages. Imagine a community that has climbed the pyramid, has tackled homelessness, literacy, and joblessness only to find they are out of water or power. (Believe it or not, as I write this paragraph the power in my office went out.)

Sustainability, at its foundation, is about survival. Without clean water, clean air, and protective infrastructures, our communities will fail just as the communities of the Dust Bowl failed. In this section you will be introduced to Huber's hierarchy of community needs pyramid—sustainability, which focuses on infrastructure and environmental needs. We address how the principles in this book can play a role in assuring not only a healthy and thriving community, but also one that can sustain itself. We will propose that the purpose-based library can play a critical and proactive role in their community's sustainability.

NOTES

1. "Dust Bowl," History.com, www.history.com/topics/dust-bowl.
2. "Quotes About Past," www.goodreads.com/quotes/tag/past.
3. Brad Plumer, "How Long Before the Great Plains Runs Out of Water?" *Washington Post, Wonkblog*, September 12, 2013, www.washingtonpost.com/blogs/wonkblog/wp/2013/09/12/how-long-before-the-midwest-runs-out-of-water.

22

Structural and Environmental Sustainability

T HROUGHOUT THIS BOOK WE HAVE ESTABLISHED HOW LOCAL libraries can become the focal point of community transformation by using Huber's hierarchy of community needs pyramid and dashboard metrics. We argue that the archival and information organizational skills of libraries are perfectly aligned with the concept of community organizational knowledge. We propose that libraries should be the keeper of the keys to this organizational knowledge and therefore position themselves as an indispensable resource to their community. We predict by following this path library funding will become a priority for city managers and community leaders. However, the issue of sustainability must not be ignored. As issues of sustainability move to the forefront of our conversations, libraries may once again find themselves left out of the conversation and the subsequent decisions of library-funding priority.

In this chapter we examine how our communities have changed over the years and how libraries have adapted along the way. We propose that libraries must continue to adapt as issues of sustainability move to the forefront of our community issues. We argue that the concepts and methodology of this book can also be applied to the issues of community sustainability. We present a new pyramid and example dashboard metrics to help guide the way. Finally we examine how your local library can lead by example and by "walking the walk" on community sustainability.

In the past 100 years we have seen a transition from urban-centered communities to expansive suburban communities. We have seen a transition from farming communities to industrial communities and now to service communities. Libraries have adapted along the way. How libraries were funded also changed. One hundred years ago, populations were centered in urban cities where the population-to-land ratio was large. The infrastructure to support these cities could be better leveraged within a tighter geographical area than in a sprawling one. Funding for a few libraries was not of concern. As the communities spread out to larger geographical areas, the infrastructure to support these communities (roads, water, electric, and sewer) became more expensive. However, in a good economy, funds for libraries were still available. What funding challenges will the next 100 years bring? We can all hope that this economy is not the new normal and that good times are around the corner. Nonetheless, we can predict that sustainability issues will continue to grow. As we discussed in prior chapters, in today's economy, you might hear city managers say, "Do we cut funding to firefighters and police or do we cut funding to libraries?" In the next 100 years, the conversation will most likely be "Do we want to cut funding for infrastructure needs that provide clean water, clean transportation, and effective sewage treatment, or do we cut library funding?" To stay relevant, not only must libraries be a part of the conversation on community transformation, they must also be seen as part of the solution for community sustainability.

Mention the need for sustainable clean water, clean air, and abundant energy and you will quickly wade into the politics of climate change. However, libraries can help change the conversation by once again playing a neutral role in the political wars. Libraries can accomplish this by teaching lessons from the past and by establishing and presenting dashboard metrics on the sustainability of their communities. As we have repeated a number of times, if you do not measure it, it must not be important. To create a foundation to build our metrics upon we must once again establish our hierarchy of needs but this time for the sustainability of our community. Figure 22.1 presents Huber's hierarchy of community needs pyramid—sustainability.

At the base of our pyramid we establish our basic needs of clean and abundant water, clean air, and healthy food sources. Once our basic needs are established, our larger needs of reliable energy sources, reliable waste renewal, effective transportation, and communication must be addressed.

We have already established throughout this book how critical libraries are to the overall health and well-being of our communities. Huber's hierarchy of community needs pyramid and dashboard metrics allows libraries to show just how valuable they are. Nearly every chapter in this book could be

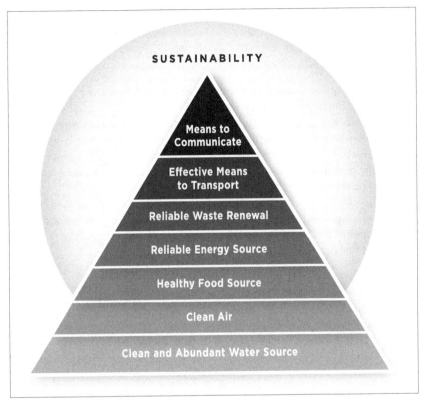

FIGURE 22.1
Huber's hierarchy of community needs—sustainability

rewritten with the sustainability pyramid in mind and it would have the same relevance. Libraries can be the keeper of the keys, collecting key community metrics, educating the public, and creating awareness of immediate and long-term issues that must be addressed. Libraries cannot wait until these issues meet emergency status, for once that has occurred, libraries might very well be left behind.

Cities are already moving in this direction of sustainability metrics. An article from Politico.com provides some examples.

> Big cities and rural communities alike are facing the perfect storm: aging infrastructure, the threat of increasingly severe and frequent weather events, and tight budgets with little to no congressional action. . . . Recognizing the need to build stronger communities, eight cities, including Milwaukee, El Paso, and Honolulu, are partnering with the Re.Invest

Initiative [which brings together technical experts and aligns public resources with private investment] to create more resilient infrastructure and build comprehensive city plans. While city action plans are not unique, the focus on data and evaluation in the Re.Invest Initiative is.[1]

The article points out that the communities are also measuring the improvements from these efforts, such as decreased energy use, increased water treatment efficiency, and community engagement. We are not proposing that libraries play a role in evaluating or creating solutions for our larger infrastructural issues, but we are suggesting libraries become the keeper of the keys in the community's sustainability dashboard metrics, including community engagement.

While the issues of sustainability can be seen (and are argued) at the global level, the solutions are at the local level. In fact, the solutions reside in the homes of your community members. As such we propose the following dashboard metrics:

- Number of energy saving programs hosted by library
- Number of households that have completed an energy assessment profile
- Total electric energy use per person in our community
- Total natural gas use per person in our community
- Number of households that have completed a water conservation profile
- Total water consumption usage per person in our community
- Number of households that have completed a recycling profile
- Number of households in our community recycling
- Number of home gardening programs hosted by library
- Number of home gardens in our community
- Number of households achieving rebates for energy conservation in our community

Furthermore, just as we suggest that your library be physically organized to represent the community pyramid, including for example the Community Transformation Center and the Children's Literacy Center, we also see the opportunity for a Community Sustainability Center surrounded by educational resources on community conservation.

In addition to helping monitor the dashboards, libraries can lead by example. By looking internally and initiating your own sustainability efforts, you gain the experience required to understand what metrics should be tracked, what actions should be taken, and what areas should become priorities. By walking the walk your library can show the community firsthand how to make a difference. Below, Steve walks us through an assessment of his own library and the actions they have taken toward improved sustainability.

POTTER'S PERSPECTIVE, POINTS, AND PONDERINGS

Library energy conservation is not a new concept. Since the oil embargo of the seventies we have been aware of the importance of reducing our energy bills. With the recent economy and the impact on our library budgets, saving money on energy bills rather than through staff cuts makes all the more sense. In this final chapter of our book I share with you some of the topics we are discussing as well as plans and actions we are taking at Mid-Continent Public Library to reduce our energy and maintenance costs.

First, we considered what upgrades MCPL could undertake to operate in a more sustainable way. Solar panels and wind turbines are still expensive and can take many years to earn back the investment. We considered something smaller, like changing traditional florescent lights to T-8 (or more efficient) ballasts. Even better, we are considering whether to migrate to LED lighting. In either case, energy costs will be dramatically decreased. But we will also gain the advantage of much less harsh lighting and creating a more pleasant and less headache-inducing environment for our customers.

For many years, windows and natural light were the natural enemies of librarians. Windows create large areas that require additional attention, more heat in the winter, and drawn shades in the summer. Windows take up important wall space that could be used for wall shelving. Library designers frequently saw windows as nothing more than a liability. Sometimes windows would leak. Sometimes windows became a security liability, with people throwing library materials out. Ultimately, when windows worked as they should, they still let in too many UV rays, bleaching out books and otherwise causing harm to library materials. But things really have changed. Multiple panes of glass and tinting combat the UV damage and buffer against the cold and heat. But more important, natural light creates a more desirable library space. Finally, traditional skylights or Solatubes can bring a lot of natural light to the center of the building. (The Carnegie Library of Pittsburgh is a great example of a library built at the dawn of electricity that uses skylights to light their stacks area when daylight is available.) There are even skylights with mirrors that follow the sun across the sky to maximize the light in a building. With the advances in building materials, there are many reasons to embrace natural light in our buildings. Not only will it make our library more desirable for people to visit, it will likely be more cost-effective to operate.

Heating and air conditioning systems become less efficient as they age. Preventive maintenance is very important. But it was also important for MCPL to change out older, less efficient systems. It is surprising how much we have lowered operation costs with more efficient HVAC equipment. In the areas where we could not afford to replace the furnace and air conditioning systems, we installed programmable thermostats and building environmental control systems. We power down the furnaces by 10 degrees overnight and fire things back up an hour before staff arrives. Why heat and cool a building when no one is there?

Many local utilities have rebate programs to help with the cost of programs like these. Rebate programs frequently encourage the installation of occupancy sensors for rooms or dimmers in the stacks. This technology will dim or turn off lights when people are not in a room or area. Sometimes the dimmers will also decrease the use of lighting when natural light is at a certain level of brightness. Have you ever thought how much money you spend lighting empty rooms? We have, and we have acquired savings and rebates as a result.

Next, we planted native and natural plantings. We do not have to water as much as a result. Not only do we save on water and pesticide costs, it is a great way to demonstrate and educate your community on native and natural plants. We consider it a different type of adult programming series.

Finally, we considered how we operate every day. The US Green Building Council administers the Leadership in Energy and Environmental Design (LEED) rating systems. Many cities have adopted design standards that encourage sustainability. In fact, it isn't uncommon to build to LEED standards just by following the building requirements in your town. But do you have to have your building certified LEED to support sustainability? Not at all. In fact, some might argue that the additional money a public entity pays to be officially LEED certified only drains money from the mission. As an independent political entity, MCPL has been slowly adopting their own operational standards that encourage sustainable operations. If a library creates standards and models behavior that everyone in the community can replicate, what better way to build a sustainable community?

Another area libraries can join the conversation is in the reuse of legacy infrastructure. People are finding their way back to downtown communities as well as their older suburban communities. The good news is the infrastructure from the past is a workable solution for the future. Several groups have advocated for the adaptive reuse of legacy infrastructure. If we cannot relocate our shuttered schools to the exurbs, can we look to convert them to maintenance-free condominiums for active seniors? There is something poetic about that. Rather than create new residential communities from former farm fields, why not re-plat and rebuild some of the postwar suburban communities? It is really eye opening to see developers create "new urbanism" developments that look just like the houses my grandparents owned in the prewar suburbs. What if we actually went to those areas and adaptively reused that housing stock to build new houses with all the charm of yesterday? By looking to the past we can create a new and effective future. Can libraries play a role in educating developers on the potential reuse of legacy infrastructure? Who better than the keeper of the keys of our community's past?

In summary, our message is that for the next 100 years, justifying the funding of libraries will continue to be an issue and a threat to libraries' long-term sustainability. To play an important role in this conversation, libraries must become an important part of the solution. We believe the Sustainability pyramid, dashboard metrics, and the methodology presented in this book can guide the way.

NOTE

1. Melody C. Barnes and John Bridgeland, "If Congress Won't Lead, States and Cities Will," Politico.com, August 16, 2013, www.politico.com/story/2013/08/if-congress-wont-lead-states-and-cities-will-95493.html#ixzz2ciZ3jrJV.

Epilogue

S TEVE AND I WOULD LIKE TO THANK YOU FOR JOINING US ON this journey. If you made it all the way to the conclusion, it shows your commitment to the survival, success, and growth of libraries.

Steve and I know we do not have all the answers, but it is our hope that this book will provide the framework for more and more discussion on the future of libraries. In 2014 I unveiled the concepts of this book at the Texas Library Association in San Antonio and subsequently have presented the concepts to many library systems. The feedback I have received has been electric. Library leaders across the country are looking for a means to focus their community transformation efforts based on value-added metrics, and they see the pyramid as the vehicle to do so.

It is our hope that libraries will realize the power of their collective footprint, embrace their purpose, and together make an even greater difference in communities across North America.

About the Authors

 **JOHN J. HUBER** formed the management consulting firm of J. Huber and Associates in 1986. Focused on the tools, principles, and concepts of lean, he has dedicated his career to helping organizations dramatically improve their customer service through improved process performance. As a pioneer in the TPS/lean revolution, he has traveled the country assisting more than 100 manufacturing, distribution, retail, and library organizations transform their operations. For the library world, he has developed breakthrough ideas including the holds label solution and the no-totes delivery solution for such clients as the New York Public Library, Carnegie Library of Pittsburgh, Tulsa City-County Library, Mid-Continent Public Library, and Austin Public Library. The author of *Lean Library Management: Eleven Strategies for Reducing Costs and Improving Customer Services* (Neal-Schuman, 2011), Huber has a bachelor's degree in industrial engineering and management from Oklahoma State University and has acquired three US patents.

STEVEN V. POTTER is the library director and CEO at Mid-Continent Public Library (MCPL) in Missouri, which in 2014 was awarded the prestigious National Medal for Museum and Library Service, and an adjunct professor at University of Missouri. Steven holds a BA in history, an MA in library science, and an MPA in public administration. The MCPL system serves more than 750,000 people, has one of the nation's largest summer reading programs, and is known for their array of innovative services. MCPL is home to the Midwest Genealogy Center, one of the nation's preeminent resources for family history, providing access to almost three-quarters of a million on-site materials. MCPL's Woodneath Library Center was opened in 2013 and includes the Story Center, which houses Woodneath Press, an on-site bookmaking printer; a digital storytelling technology lab; a recording booth; and an archive of oral, written, and digital stories produced at the center.

Index